Once Upon a Time in Berks County

Reading and Berks County In Early
Newspaper Sketches From the Pages of
The Reading Eagle

Edited and Annotated by

CHARLES J. ADAMS, III

And Annotated Again by

GEORGE M. MEISER, IX

Published by
The Historical Society of Berks County

Once Upon a Time in Berks County

©2007

No part of this book may be reproduced in any
form whatsoever without written permission
of The Historical Society of Berks County,
940 Centre Ave., Reading, PA 19601

PRINTED IN THE UNITED STATES OF AMERICA

Once Upon a Time In Berks County

Edited and Annotated by
Charles J. Adams III
And Annotated Again by
George M. Meiser IX

This book represents many hours of scrolling through microfilmed issues of the *Reading Eagle*, culling interesting illustrations, copying them, stacking the copies (in a pile that reached about eight inches in height), scanning them, and reproducing as best possible for publication.

They appear with all their warts and quirks, many of them scrubbed electronically and removed of major scratches, smudges, and shading inherent with the process of microfilming century-old newspapers.

Certain levels of clarity may have been compromised in the transferal of these illustrations to these pages.

Also included among the historically-significant sketches and anecdotes are examples of vintage advertising from the period of roughly 1895-1910.

The result is a unique compilation of random sketches and drawings and summaries of the captions or stories that appeared with them, as provided by author and Historical Society of Berks County board member Charles J. Adams III.

Mr. Adams then turned the pages over to Berks County historian and Historical Society President George M. Meiser IX, who reviewed all pictures and text and re-annotated them. If certain items needed correction, clarification, or amplification, Mr. Meiser drew from his vast knowledge and resources to enhance the original material.

The intent of this volume is to present glimpses into the turn-of-the-20th century Berks County as seen through the eyes and hands of the talented newspaper artists who chronicled with their pens that era of unprecedented growth.

The illustrations herein will hopefully spark your imagination, bring out a chuckle or two, and perhaps even tease your memories.

Much of what is in the following pages has fallen to progress, nature, disaster, or time. Quaint and curious traditions and lifestyles and splendid structures seen here have simply disappeared.

But, imagine a Berks County when steamboats chugged on the Schuylkill...when streetcars took passengers to ball games and amusement parks...when new homes and office buildings were opened almost daily...and when those sketch artists toiled to record it all for *Reading Eagle* readers to enjoy.

It happened Once Upon a Time in Berks County.

The Historical Society of Berks County will receive the proceeds from the sale of this book.

1896: A Building Boom in Reading!

New buildings were springing up throughout the city in 1896, and the newspaper dedicated a full two pages to the boom.

On this page, clockwise from top left, we see the new Girls' High School at 4th and Court Streets, the Wanner Building, Reed and Court Streets; the Bissinger Office Building, 606 Court Street; and the Pearson Building, 619 Penn Street. The Bissinger building was erected by Philip Bissinger and included the offices of the law firm of O'Reilly & Deysher, the office of Atty. Charles M. Plank, and several other law offices. The entire second floor was occupied by the Americus Club, which included a parlor, reading room, and billiard room.

The Pearson Building served as the headquarters of the Great Atlantic & Pacific Tea Company.

On the next page, clockwise from top left: the Second National Bank Building, the Bright & Lerch Building, 504 Penn Street; the Rodgers Building, 402 Penn Street; and the new Mansion House Hotel, on the southeast corner of 5th and Penn Streets.

"Some of the structures are not only magnificent in proportions, but really elegant in design, solidly and substantially built, and reflect great credit on the enterprise of the owners and the high ability of Reading's architects, builders, contractors, carpenters, and other skilled workers, and would draw attention and admiration were they to stand among the handsome buildings of larger cities."

In 1904, the *Reading Eagle* published this sketch of the first Pennsylvania Railroad depot, which stood at the foot of Penn Street in Reading. The sketch was actually made from a picture taken on November 21, 1884.

They were called "double-headers," those Baldwin locomotives that operated on the Reading Company's lines in suburban Philadelphia. They were unique in that they were combination locomotives and tenders, with cowcatchers on both ends. The curious locomotives were put into service by the Reading in 1903.

An "open car" typical of those that operated on the United Traction Co.'s city lines in Reading in 1901.

The Stewart, Newberger & Co. cigar manufacturers, at 616 N. 8th St. in 1904, packed this freight car with a quarter of a million stogies made in their plant and destined for a distributor in Scranton.

Ever Vigilant...

There once were watchmen at the Penn Street railroad crossing at 7th Street. And, they became local heroes as they kept vigil at the busy intersection where cars, trains, and people converged.

At right is John D. Schantz, depicted in a 1905 sketch. Schantz kept thorough diaries of weather conditions at his post, was a friend to both pedestrians and engineers, and was a loyal Reading Railroad employee for many years. He would keep the tracks and sidewalks around his watch box clean and free of snow, and was a familiar sight waving his red flag to the trainmen and lowering the crossing gates for the walking and wheeled traffic.

Below, Henry Keller is seen at the same 7th and Penn watch box in 1898. "He is always in the best of spirits," an *Eagle* article said of him, "and greets his friends and acquaintances with a hearty 'Good morning.' The trainmen also have a warm spot for Mr. Keller, and he is invariably greeted by the men in the cab and caboose as the trains pass."

"The life of a watchman at 7th and Penn is not an easy berth because you are kept busy from the time you go on duty until you leave. Trains are passing all day and the gates must be lowered and raised every time. The work of lifting them is not hard and I have gotten used to it long ago. I am on my feet most of the time, but in bad weather, snow and hail, I use the watch box along the track. If I could only get people to keep back and not continually risk their lives by running across the tracks in front of the express trains! It often seems to be that these people don't mind the delay caused by a long coal train, but they can't spare enough time to stand half a minute to allow an express to go by.

--Henry Keller, 1898

Henry W. Burkey was the watchman at the Pear and Washington Street railroad crossing in 1903, and he gave his watch box side yard a personal touch by planting petunias, asters, and dozens of other flowers in a pleasant garden (below) that provided the neighborhood with a little color and Burkey with something to do in between train crossings.

Meanwhile, at the 3rd and Walnut Sts. crossing, watchman John E. Frey installed a flag staff (above) with climbing vines as the centerpiece of his watch box garden. Unique in his plot were the nearly three dozen corn stalks that were on the perimeter of the plot.

Fillin' 'er up...1915 style.

A 54-foot long street railway car (left) was the pride of the United Traction Company's Oley Valley Railway line in 1901. The car could hustle passengers from Reading to Oley at a 40 miles per hour clip! Depicted below is a car that took folks on the Womelsdorf Branch of the railway.

In 1907, prospective buyers were lured to the new "Rosedale Addition" housing development with 6-cent rides on the Temple Line of the railway company.

BRIGHT & COMPANY,
504-506 PENN ST., READING.
—HEADQUARTERS FOR—
HARDWARE, IRON and STEEL BUILDING MATERIAL,
PAINTS, OILS, GLASS, Etc.
HOUSEFURNISHING GOODS.
STOVES and HEATERS.
AGATE and TINWARE.
······CUTLERY······
Large line of SPORTING GOODS, 2d floor front.

Designed in Reading

Mechanical engineer of the Reading railroad shops, F.F. Gaines, designed this fast ~~freight~~ Passenger locomotive that rolled into service in October, 1905. It was one of five that served on the Allentown-to-Harrisburg main line.

Sending a Clear Signal...

This 1902 array of sketches depicts three crucial switch towers on the Belt Line of the P&R Railroad. At left is the Cumru Junction tower. It was equipped with ten levers and regulated signals and switches for trains that went on the old Wilmington & Northern tracks to Birdsboro, and then onto the Main Line. Below, left, is the 35-lever tower that switched trains between the Belt Line and Main Line north of the city, as well as trains on the Schuylkill and Lehigh Branch. Below, right, is the Klapperthal Junction tower, a 15-lever facility. The men there were in charge of regulating all traffic running northward over the Belt Line.

In 1902, the Berkshire Country Club began construction on this elaborate swimming pavilion and bath house on the west bank of the river. The club was also building its golf course, and its club house was in the planning stages. The Berkshire swimming area was located south of the Reading Swimming Club pool. Note the boat landing in front of the bath house.

The Schuylkill River was once veritably lined with boathouses, docks, landings, and clubhouses. The 1902 drawing at left shows one of several private clubhouses built by consortiums of families or companies and used as summer retreats. The structure at left was situated on "Boyer's Island," just south of the Bingaman Street Bridge.

The weather wasn't always fit for man nor boat, and boat storage sheds such as the one on the right were situated along the river bank from the Bingaman Street Bridge to Klapperthal and other points along the Schuylkill.

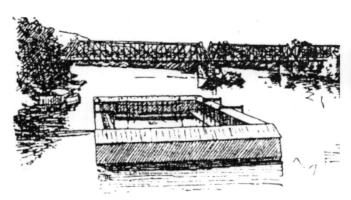

That's the old Bingaman Street Bridge in the background, and that's the Reading Turn Verein's 110x40-foot swimming pool right, smack dab in the middle of the Schuylkill River. Some 500 swimmers could be accommodated in the pool, and could avail themselves of 32 private dressing rooms in a pavilion on the shore. Price of admission–a dime for adults, a nickel for kids. The year–1895.

Canals

Yes, sternwheelers once plied the Schuylkill River in Reading! Once called the "John Smith," the steamboat seen in this 1903 drawing was renamed the "City of Reading." Owned by the Reading Steamboat Assn., the vessel took passengers on excursions between Kissinger's and Hain's Locks, a distance of about two miles.

More than 100 members of the Schuylkill Fire Company formed the Harmony Social Club in 1901, and maintained its clubhouse in this flat-bottom boat that was moored at the near the confluence of the Tulpehocken Creek and Schuylkill River. It was towed there from its original mooring spot just south of the Bingaman Street Bridge, where it was owned by the Bijou Social Club. The Harmony club purchased it for $100 and made many improvements.

A variety of pleasure boats were anchored in the waters of the Schuylkill in 1899, including the "Monitor," which was owned by Bert Shanaman. It was possible at the time to take a boat down the river as far as Philadelphia.

In 1903, legendary steamboat and canal boat captain John A. Hiester established a park at his steamboat landing at the foot of S. 6th Street. His boats, the "Rosie" and the "Atlantic," carried large numbers of passengers on excursions on the Schuylkill River between his landing and High's Woods, several miles downstream.

Upstream, the Reading Boat Club and other boating and canoeing clubs created a "Boathouse Row" that stretched along the riverbanks from the North Reading Locks of the Schuylkill Canal beyond the Berkshire Country Club. Some 160 boats were in the water in that section of the river, according to a 1903 *Eagle* story.

The "Willow Grove" park, adjacent to Hiester's Boat Landing, was a popular place for river swimming in 1903. This picture shows the "Shoot-the-Chute" sliding board that sent daring swimmers careening into a deep part of the Schuylkill. The grounds of the park were neatly groomed, laced with gravel paths, graced by many picnic benches, shaded by tall trees, and included bath houses for the swimmers.

The Hills Were Alive...

It was described as a "side issue" of the Reading Aerie No. 66, Fraternal Order of Eagles. It was their Mountain Home Assn. on Mount Penn, and it was hailed by Eagles' aeries far and wide as a model for clubhouses everywhere.

Now "Liederkrantz"

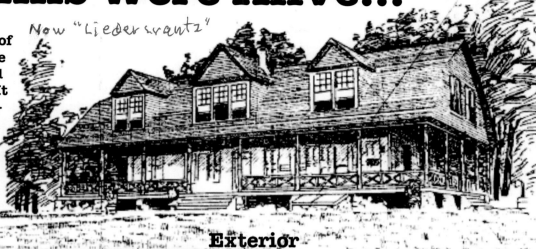

Exterior

Interior

Sausage Grinders, Stuffers, Lard Presses, Cutlery, Etc.

Best Quality for Least Money.

STICHTER'S Hardware Store,

505-509 PENN ST., READING

Horse Blankets

Big stock. All grades and prices.

J. H. Obold & Co.
—HARDWARE—
3d and PENN.

Another addition to Mt. Penn in 1903 was the Mountain Spring Assn. club house. The club had been formed in 1891, and purchased two acres on the mountain. Its first structure was a small cottage. In 1892, the club sold 25 shares at $100 each, built the clubhouse, a pond stocked with trout, and a shady grove. The original clubhouse included a sun parlor, reading room stocked with magazines and newspapers, and a large dining room. The association also had its own carriages, a horse, 100 chickens, and a goat named "Short Light."

WHITNER'S DAYLIGHT STORE

New Fall Kid Gloves

We are ready with every correct style in gloves suitable for street, dress and evening wear, including the new 16-button length Mousquetaire in black or white at $2.75.

Special attention is directed to the new stock of our P. L. 2-clasp glove at $1.00. This glove has been our leader at $1.00 for a good many years, and to our mind there is no doubt that it is the best glove value that $1.00 will buy. We are so sure of its goodness that we give a very strong guarantee with each pair. All the staple shades including black and white.

Fownes' Eugenie two-clasp Glace, Paris point stitching, at $1.50. | Fownes' English Walking Gloves, $1.50. Dents' 2-clasp Real Kid, $1.50.

New LaVida Corsets Are Here

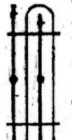

The fashionable figure has changed and LaVida corsets will reduce your figure to the new fashion without the least discomfort.

The wearer of LaVida's not only has comfortable corsets, but corsets that will grade off any awkward spots of the person into graceful, pleasing lines.

LaVida corsets are filled with pure whalebone and made of the finest imported materials; they are light, springy and retain elasticity and proper outlines to the end.

Many models, a perfect fit for any figure, $3.50 to $11.00.

C. K. WHITNER & CO.

Wrought Iron Fencing PLAIN AND ORNAMENTAL

Fire Escapes, Step and Area Railings, Window Guards and General Building Iron Work. Structural Work. Beams and Channels in Stock.

BOTH 'PHONES. ESTIMATES and DESIGNS PROMPTLY FURNISHED

W. F. Remppis, Co.
WATER ST. ABOVE LANCASTER BRIDGE. READING, PA.

SECOND-HAND PIANOS
for sale, cheap. Some slightly used. $20 to $100.
ARTHUR WITTICH, - 116 S. SIXTH ST.

HOLIDAY GOODS.

THE GRANDEST DISPLAY IN READING.
Diamonds, Watches, Jewelry, Silverware, Clocks, Leather Goods, Cut Glass, Hand-Painted China, Umbrellas, Etc.

SCHLECHTER'S, 428 Penn St.

And, That Scar on Mt. Penn?

Still visible on the western slope of Mt. Penn are the remains of the Mt. Penn Sand and Stone Company quarry, operated by E.C. Kirschman. Steam engines, boilers, a stone crusher, and a 600-foot long narrow gauge rail line were once situated there, run by 22 men and six horses.

"The large quarry cannot be seen from the front of the city and by no means destroys the pretty view of the mountain." -- **1905**

Twins on the Hill...

"Favorable to the location of the two houses of worship is the fact that they will stand on a knoll which commands an elegant view of the city, country, and mountain, and which will also make them visible for miles around, especially from Mt. Penn. It is ideal."

With those words in its February 24, 1907, edition, the *Reading Eagle* noted the plans to replace the "ancient" Alsace Union Church with two churches along Kutztown Road.

"When they are completed, they may not have their parallel for interest in the United States. The charming sight will be one of the special prides of old Berks"

The churches were planned to be virtually identical, except for the positioning of the Sunday School chapels, owing to the lay of the land atop the hill. The estimated costs of the buildings—including all furnishings—was between $35,000 and $40,000.

"The career of the union church will be perpetuated by erecting the new edifices on the same hallowed ground. Her history will therefore be conserved."

...and Twins in the Valley

In the Oley Valley in 1898 were the virtually identical twin churches of Christ Lutheran (left) and Oley Reformed. They stood about 150 yards apart along the Oley Turnpike near Spangsville. Although quite alike, the Reformed church was built of brick and the Lutheran was native stone. Both buildings traced their roots to a log meeting house built on the site in 1735. Reformed and Lutheran congregations shared that small building. In 1821, the Lutherans built their new church and the following year, the Reformed congregation built theirs.

...and Towers in the Town

An energetic article in the May 16, 1897 newspaper provided views and statistics about the tallest structures in Reading. It was long before any commercial or government building rose, and the six tallest towers in town were the spires of churches. The seventh highest was the Berks County Court House. Above, from left: Trinity Lutheran, 201 feet, 7 inches; Christ Cathedral, 197 feet; First Reformed, 189 feet; St. Paul's Catholic, 187 feet; St. John's Lutheran, 183 feet; St. Peter's Catholic, 147 feet; and the county court house, 142 feet.

The belfry and bell at Hinnershitz Church in Tuckerton were brand new in October, 1899, and about 1,500 people came from all over the county to watch the dedication and hear the musical tributes offered by the Epler's and Leesport church choirs under the direction of J.B. Ammarell. An account of the dedication of the belfry and bell noted that trains brought many to the event, and "Breidegam's Hotel was crowded with guests." The bell weighed 1,820 pounds and was placed in a belfry that towered 65 feet. In the inset is Catharine Maurer, who was the benefactor of the bell and belfry, in memory of her deceased parents.

At left is the 350-seat funeral chapel in Fairview Cemetery in Boyertown at the time of its opening in 1905.

In 1895, the congregation of Tulpehocken Trinity Reformed Church (right) celebrated its 150th anniversary. The Rev. Thomas M. Yundt of Womelsdorf (inset) delivered the sermon. Just west of Stouchsburg, the church was also known as "Leinbach's Church," as the Revs. Thomas H. and Charles Leinbach were its pastors for more than 50 years.

Places to Stay....

(ABOVE) This was the architect's rendering of a new hotel to be built on the northwest corner of 7th and Franklin Sts. in 1904. Described as a "first class hotel" mainly for travelers, the operation was to be operated by brewing magnate John Barbey and replace an earlier hotel on the site operated by Prof. John A. Fahrbach.

(BELOW) The "improved" Highland House on Neversink Mountain, seen in a 1906 view. The property had recently been purchased by Dr. John Y. Hoffman, who plowed much money into what was an almost complete renovation. Visitors from places such as Atlantic City, Philadelphia, New York City, and all points came to enjoy the hotel. Also featured were Sunday evening dinners and Wednesday and Saturday evening music with dinner, aimed at the local trade.

H.N. and W.S. SCHWARTZ'S "Mt. Penn Summit Hotel" was located about 125 feet south of the Tower atop Mt. Penn. At 93-feet high, the hotel was actually taller than the Tower.

"The hotel will certainly prove an attractive feature to the already delightful ride over the Mt. Penn Gravity R.R. and will undoubtedly be a factor in drawing strangers to Reading."

The hotel featured a large dining room, an antique oak bar, several "sleeping apartments," and wrap-around porches.

"Views from these 16-foot wide verandahs afford a promenade 828 feet in length. From them are visible the church steeples of Lebanon, the furnaces at Robesonia and Sheridan, and Wernersville, with the mountain resorts plainly visible."

"Adjoining the Summit Hotel are many romantic walks which are being put into excellent condition, and the hotel is also accessible by the Hill Road drive."

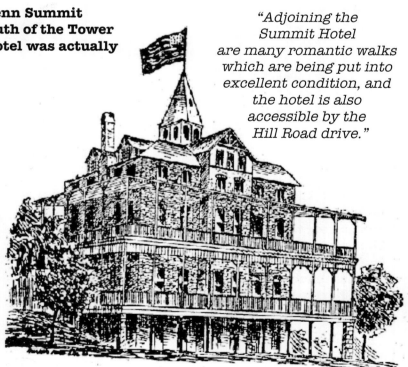

...Places to Play...

A playground at 4th and Pine Sts. in Reading was brand new in 1903, and it rapidly became a gathering spot for the children of that section of town. Construction of the playground was made possible by a fundraising effort by the Civic League, and the Civic Division of the Woman's Club agreed to manage and maintain it.

"The see-saws are occupied all day. One is for the use of the smaller children. It is fitted out with handles and a patent balancer. Some of the older children sit under the grape arbor for hours reading and watching the others play. The entire playground is shaded by many large fruit trees."

The Civic League made it a project to establish playgrounds in several neighborhoods throughout the city, with the intention of having the city take them over if they proved successful.

In 1906, the P&R Railroad's YMCA grounds at N. 6th and Oley Sts. included a baseball grounds and a pair of lawn tennis courts (left).

"Lovers of the game can be seen there every afternoon and evening. The grounds were filled with earth and then rolled. They are said to be fully as good as any in the city or the suburbs."

...and Places to Pray

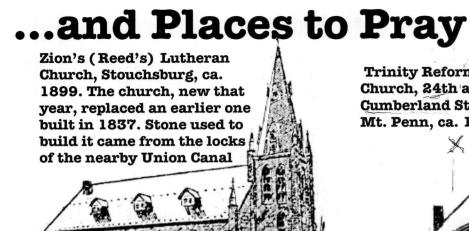

Zion's (Reed's) Lutheran Church, Stouchsburg, ca. 1899. The church, new that year, replaced an earlier one built in 1837. Stone used to build it came from the locks of the nearby Union Canal

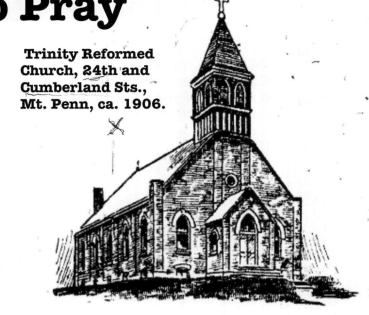

Trinity Reformed Church, 24th and Cumberland Sts., Mt. Penn, ca. 1906.

Congregation Shomro Habrith Synagogue, ca. 1913. Located on N. 8th St. between Green and Greenwich Sts., this Gothic-style edifice was built with a buff shade of Pompeian brick, ornamented with terra cotta trimmings and Indiana limestone arch blocks. According to published reports of the day, the structure cost $25,000 to build. The building featured a copper dome and the Ten Commandments in raised bronze letters above its doorway.

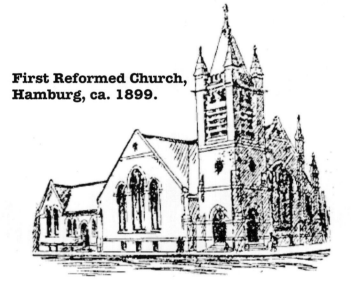

First Reformed Church, Hamburg, ca. 1899.

Bethany Union Chapel, Stony Creek Mills, ca. 1900., built at a cost of $4,500.

18

A Walk in the Park...

Pansies...thousands of them...once graced Penn's Common, and the sketch at left does its best to show one of the two beds that were planted in 1901 by city landscape gardner Charles Gindra. One pansy bed was located below the McKinley monument, while the other was directly below the lily pond.

"Mr. Gindra would have planted another on the Walnut Street side, but it would soon have been rooted up by the dogs that run about the place."

That year, Gindra also planted a two new rose patches with 18 varieties of roses, several tulip beds, and many geranium beds.

"A visit through the park greenhouse these days is a treat. It is open to visitors every Sunday afternoon, and Mr. Gindra invites inspection."

A Fountain of Youth in City Park

Hebe is the Greek goddess of youth, the daughter of Zeus and Hera. It was her image that, in an 1899 Reading Eagle article, was destined for the reservoir in Penn's Common. In fact, there would be two identical statues of the goddess there, both tossing water from a pitcher to a cup.

"It will be erected on the small plot at the head of the stairs alongside the home of the superintendent on North 11th."

"These improvements will be made at considerable expense, but it is believed that they will be appreciated by the public."

Another major work of art set to be built on the reservoir was a drinking fountain dominated by a 11-foot tall elk.

"There will be a ground basin 12 feet, six inches octagon, the latter being intended for gold and silver fish."

"The height to the top of the eight drinking fountains is four feet, two inches. Each of the latter have two outlets and are supplied with drinking cups."

Reading's "Palm Coast"...ca. 1899

OK, it wasn't really a "coast," but in 1899, palm trees were planted in Reading's Penn's Commons park. At right is the "Floral Star" and palm near the lily pond. Below is the geranium bed which was highlighted by a palm tree or two. Just beyond the arrangement is the old spring house in the park.

The newspaper called them "Living Floral Pictures" in the park, and they included this floral shield near the greenhouse.

"The above are a few scenes of beauty in the City Park. They are "living pictures" worth seeing. Those who most frequently drive, ride, or stroll through the park are loudest in their praise. Go see the beauties there that are on free show every day. It will re-pay you. Morning or evening the views are ennobling. It is one of the few places in Reading where taxpayers can see where their money goes. The floral pictures all over the park are artistic and well done, and everything is in good shape."

Strike Up the Band!

Before the bandshell there was a much simpler band stand in City Park. The 1897 version was designed by City Parks Commissioner Philip Bissinger, who said it was inspired by band stands he noticed in several European cities during a trip in 1896.

"It is octagonal in shape, 27 feet in diameter and 28 feet in height. It is built of iron and wood, the supports being of iron resembling knights' lances with ornamental heads."

"The Finest Bicycle Oval in this Section of the United States"

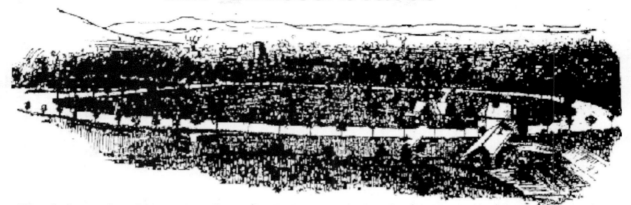

That's how the newspaper described the nearly half-mile long, "wide, hard, and smooth," bicycle track in City Park in 1897.

"It is a most charming and delightful track, of which our bicyclists are justly proud. Visitors are simply carried away with a view of it. Five hundred people on wheels would not crowd the oval at all. Bicycling in such cool, pure, fresh air, as is to be had in the park, surrounded by all the beauties of nature, is certainly a rare exercise which cannot be too highly appreciated."

A floral urn (left), a Maltese Cross (below), and a shamrock were among the floral art in City Park in 1897.

Before the Anchor in City Park...

...There was an Anchor in City Park

It may be difficult to discern in the sketch at left, but that's a ship's anchor made of a bed of flowers. In 1897, the floral arrangement was planted near the park reservoir.

...and Before the Cannonballs...
...There Was This:

April 15, 1906: Credit the Civic League for the transformation of what had been a hideous pole-storing plot of ground at N. 5th St. and Centre Ave. into a nicely landscaped park. The woman's club purchased the land and donated it to the city for park purposes.

"It will be made one of the most beautiful of the several similar plots now owned by the city. Efforts are now being made to raise money to construct a coping about the plot. After it has been graded and sodded, it will be beautified by the P&R Co.'s landscape gardener."

The city hoped the beautification of the half-acre, triangular plot would complement a nearby plot bounded by Centre Ave., Douglass and Fourth Sts. and add a bit of green to what was then the fringe of center-city Reading.

1900: The Changing Face of a City

An impressive spurt of growth in the city of Reading in 1900 was chronicled by the *Reading Eagle* in a full-page layout of renderings of new construction projects. Clockwise, from upper left: The new annex of the Dives, Pomeroy & Stewart department store along S. 6th St.; the store's annex on the Penn St. side; The new "Woodward St. Market" east of N. 5th between Buttonwood and Woodward Sts.; the new United Transportation and Power Co.'s car barns at 10th and Exeter (with a capacity of 130 cars); and the new W.H. Luden's candy factory at 8th and Elm Sts.

**Other projects that grabbed the public's attention in 1900 included (above) the new Hershey Building, on Penn St. just east of 8th St., which was to be a candy factory.
The Shade & Sons store (top right) built a new addition to its facility on Penn above 6th St., and in the suburbs, the Montello Brick Works erected a massive plant in Wyomissing (below).** Glen-Gery

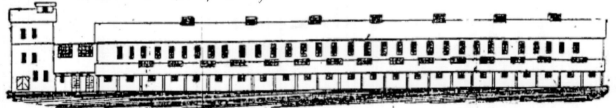

The Artist at Work...

The artist was the renowned Ben Austrian, seen at right with his new (October, 1899) work, "A Day's Hunt." The caption of the sketch offered an unusual admission:

"Mr. Austrian is supposed to be standing aside of his now famous work, but the drawing of his face is not a good likeness. The rest of the picture is all right."

The work was uniquely multimedia, with actual shutters and hinges and painted game.

"People stand puzzled before the painting, unable to tell where reality leaves off and art begins. The astonishing effectiveness of the work is, of course, the strong contrast between the rudeness of the shutter and the beauty of the game. What appears to be fur is just paint."

At right is Austrian's "His Majesty, The King," done in 1904. The work was displayed at the Dives, Pomeroy & Stewart store for two weeks, but was taken to Green's Hotel, Philadelphia, whose owner, M.W. Newton, paid $4,500 for it.

Where Elks Once Gathered...

In May, 1904, the Reading Lodge No. 115, Order of Elks, occupied what was formerly the Horatio Trexler Mansion at 5th and Franklin Sts. in downtown Reading. According to a story published at the time, the mansion (which cost a then-whopping $87,000 to build in the early 1870s), stood on the site of a log school building where Polly Babb and Mr. and Mrs. John Taylor once taught.

The Elks pledged to spend up to $5,000 to renovate the property for its needs. One of the first orders of business was to erect a ten-foot high, 1,600-pound, bronze elk statue that would adorn the corner of the grounds.

The Elks made extensive improvements, including creating a sitting room with a Turkish flair, installing a tap room, and a "jolly room" with card tables and other items "fitted out for the comfort of the members."

In 1906, the Elks allocated $40,000 for a large addition to their home, extending along Franklin Street, as seen in the drawing below. The extension included sleeping rooms on the third floor; a lodge room on the second; billiard tables, telephone booths, a dining room, stage, and serving rooms on the first; and four bowling alleys, a rathskeller, and shower baths in the basement. Plans also included a roof garden.

"A feature of this new addition to the Elks club house will be its furnishing," it was reported. "No expense will be spared to insure the comfort of the members."

The "Flatiron Building," Reading-style. This 1904 view of what was then the Junction House included the dimensions of the building (40 feet wide at its widest, 7 feet wide at its narrowest). The item said the building was erected "over 40 years ago" by Daniel Zwoyer. It also noted that the Hampden Fire Co. was organized in the hall of the building which, in 1904, was owned by the Reading Brewing Company. It stands, oddly enough, at the corner of N. 8th and N. 9th Sts.

The "New Armory," circa 1887. Built on the site of the old Metropolitan Rink on the east side of S. 5th St. near Chestnut, the 68-feet high structure included a drill room, banquet halls, and various offices. Its construction cost was $31,000.

The Meeting Room (left) and Reading Room of the offices of the Reading Board of Trade, after extensive alterations in 1904. The offices were located in the F.S. Jacobs Bldg., 25 N. 6th Street in Reading.

All's Fair In Reading...

Then as now, Berks Countians enjoy a good country fair. Pictures here are scenes from the Berks County Fair of 1904. Big attractions at the fair that year included fresh-baked pies, oyster dinners in the W.C.T.U. Restaurant, a Ferris wheel, many midway attractions, exotic animals, midway games, freak shows, horse races, many agricultural exhibits, and palm-pressing politicians. An unidentified 12-year old girl guards a 210-pound pumpkin that was put on display by Daniel R. Lenhart, of Leesport.

...and in Kutztown.

In October, 1905, the Kutztown Fair Association unveiled its plans to rebuild a fairgrounds on 30 acres of land that was formerly the Fairview stock farm. A track was built, and a 1,000-seat grandstand was built, along with a 42x100-foot fair house.

Stables (below) to accommodate 40 race horses were added, as was a judges' stand (left). When it was discovered that a suitable entrance to the fairgrounds was not available, an adjacent orchard was purchased and a proper approach to the grounds was created.

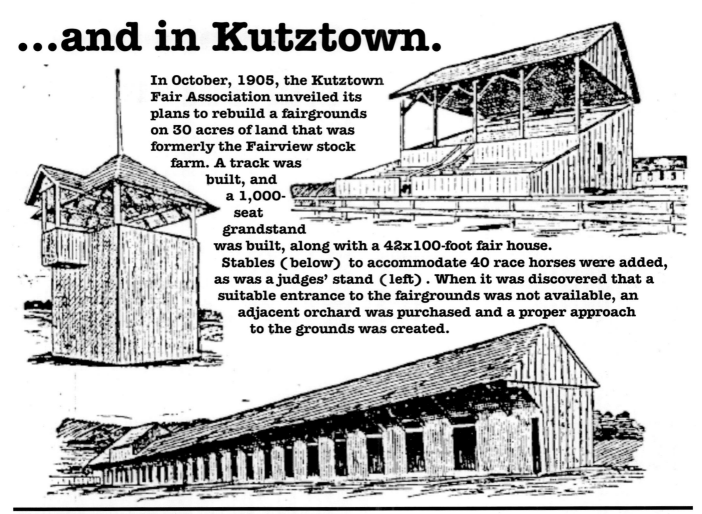

And While We're in Kutztown...

....let's have a look at the new, $30,000 gymnasium that was build at the "Keystone Normal School" (now Kutztown University) in 1907. The structure was built on the site of the school's baseball grounds and featured a 25-foot high court, a running track, a swimming tank in the basement, four bowling alleys, and all the latest athletic equipment. Offices for physical exams and the "physical director" were also included. Lighting would be provided by the windows and overhead skylights.

29

Gobblers and Gas Burners...

A young man sits with one of the big draws at the entrance to the Blandon Poultry Show in the late 1890s. The 45-pound gobbler was purchased by a Berks County farmer in Indiana and brought to the show as a curiosity. Below, men tend their gasoline engines at the Berks County Fair of 1904. The engines ranged from two to eight-horsepower and were recent additions to the farms of the county at the time.

Join the Club...

...the Berkshire Country Club, that is.

It was the summer of 1903 when the Berkshire Country Club opened just north of the city on what was once the "Jacobs farm." That farm had been purchased by George F. Baer, who sold it to the club's investors. It initially included a 3,000-yard nine-hole golf course, tennis courts, and its elegant club house. At right are representations of the Dining Room (top) and Tap Room.

The club house also featured a women's parlor, locker rooms, office, kitchens, two sleeping rooms, and nearby stables and wagon sheds.

Carsonia Park

Early views of the legendary amusement park that is now the Pennside section of Lower Alsace and Exeter Townships include the "Laughing Gallery" (1902, right) and the "Dancing Pavilion" (1905, below).

The Laughing Gallery was more commonly known as the "hall of mirrors." Ten mirrors, each six feet by 40 inches, presented different reflections of whomever stood in front of them.

It was modeled after similar attractions at Willow Grove and Chestnut Hill parks in Philadelphia, and at Kennywood Park in Pittsburgh. At all of those parks, it was the biggest moneymaker. The Carsonia building was erected and managed by Inter-State Park Amusement Co.

In 1903, Inter-State also solicited bids to erect a fence and seats at Carsonia Park.

"In this enclosure the big carnival will be held, base ball played, while the horse show, a wild west show and other big attractions will be seen there next summer."

The Dancing Pavilion was built through a stock company headed by Reading dance instructor Harold V. Drexel. The pavilion replaced a restaurant that stood on the shore of Carsonia Lake. With a stone foundation and frame construction, the "pavilion" was 70 feet high, 100 feet wide, and 170 feet long. Beneath the dance floor was a restaurant and dressing rooms.

A 40-by-30 foot stage was situated on one end of the building.

"The building will be modern throughout and will contain every feature looking to the comfort of patrons."

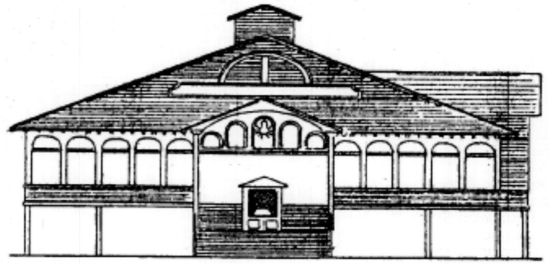

At top right is the "new $10,000 attraction" at Carsonia Park (new in 1907), the "caroussel, or merry-go-round."
The caroussel was inside a covered building just inside the main entrance near the band stand. Built for Inter-State Park Amusement Co. by the G.A. Dentzel & Sons firm of Philadelphia ("who have made a fortune out of merry-go-rounds"), the unit was surrounded by seating for 1,000 people.

"Experience has shown that the merry-go-round is the most lasting of all park attractions, and when located at a good resort it is seldom the entire cost is not realized in the first season. The receipts from a merry-go-round like the one at Carsonia have exceeded $900 in a single day."

At right, middle, is the actual "big wheel" of the "Old Mill" at Carsonia Park. Built at a cost of nearly $15,000, the "Old Mill" was considered one of the finest attractions of its kind in any park, anywhere.

"The attraction consists of, as its name implies, a complete representation of an old mill in actual operation. There's the big wheel run by actual water, the water races, etc. The real attraction is a the ride in a boat through these races, which are enclosed on both sides and top, while the bottom is a flowing stream. The ride through these races is taken on a boat holding six passengers and a series of surprises attends the ride. The ride is more than a half mile in length and requires about six minutes to make. Along the races of the old mill at Carsonia, the boat passes six interesting scenes, comprising a church with its old bells chiming; then, in a flash, the boat apparently shoots into the infernal regions with the King of Hades and his imps in active possession. Another journey in the boat of a hundred feet or more and there is seen a most beautiful moonlight ocean view showing a full-rigged ship, apparently moving silently over the moonlight-tipped waves of the sea. Suddenly the boat turns a curve in the race and the passengers find themselves in 'Davy Jones' Locker,' a realistic scene of the bottom of the ocean at a point where lovely mermaids are in convention. The next scene is the chamber of mystic mirrors."

Because There Was This...

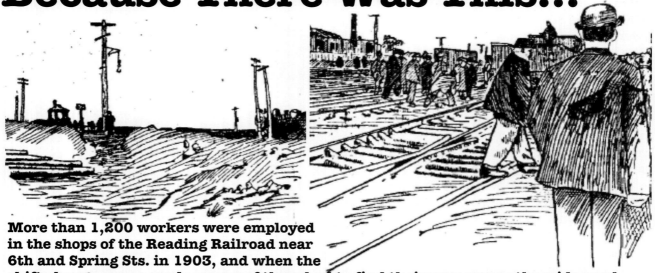

More than 1,200 workers were employed in the shops of the Reading Railroad near 6th and Spring Sts. in 1903, and when the shift changes were made, many of them had to find their way across the wide yard and streams of very active railroad tracks at the Spring St. crossing.

"There is not a day that some of the hundreds of people employed by the company do not run some risk at that crossing. There is sufficient evidence that a bridge of some kind is badly needed at that point."

...There Is This

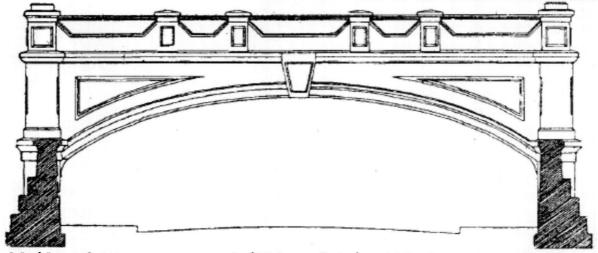

A bridge, of course, was never built there. But, in 1907, plans were released for the construction of the "Spring Street Subway," which would connect the city's northeast and northwest sections and provide safe passage for vehicles and pedestrians. Credit for the idea was given to William Abbott Witman, the legendary Reading entrepreneur and politician, who lobbied city council to raise taxes to pay for the underpass.

"There will be a retaining wall of concrete on each side of the approach. These walls will be of ornamental design as is shown in the illustration, and on each side there will be nine 25-foot panels. This will be highly appreciated by the people of the northern section of the city."

But, There Was Almost This...

Instead of a "subway" plunging beneath the 6th and Spring Sts. railroad crossing, a bridge might have soared over it, if plans by certain visionaries would have come to fruition.

The 1903 sketch above depicts a 331-foot long span that would have carried traffic over the railroad yards. The plan, obviously, was never adopted.

"People living in the northern section appear to be more largely in favor of a subway, although either one would be very welcome. While the cost of a subway, it is said, would be as great as an overhead structure, the subsequent cost of maintenance would be trifling as compared with the cost of maintaining a bridge."

In the sketch is a dotted line that shows the course of a "subway" that would have coursed under the railroad tracks in another plan—that was ultimately adopted.

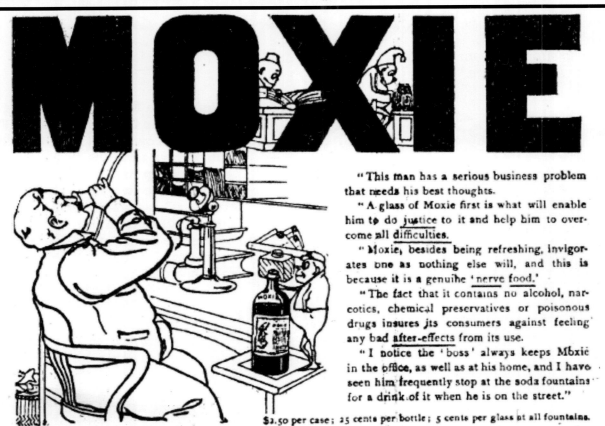

MOXIE

"This man has a serious business problem that needs his best thoughts.

"A glass of Moxie first is what will enable him to do justice to it and help him to overcome all difficulties.

"Moxie, besides being refreshing, invigorates one as nothing else will, and this is because it is a genuine 'nerve food.'

"The fact that it contains no alcohol, narcotics, chemical preservatives or poisonous drugs insures its consumers against feeling any bad after-effects from its use.

"I notice the 'boss' always keeps Moxie in the office, as well as at his home, and I have seen him frequently stop at the soda fountains for a drink of it when he is on the street."

$2.50 per case; 25 cents per bottle; 5 cents per glass at all fountains.

Huntin' 'n' Fishin' 'n' Stuff...

Elias J. Mengel, Philip M. Harner, Joel Mengel, and a dog named "Fire" are seen in this 1897 depiction of a Berks County small game hunting camp near Strausstown. The men went out for rabbit, partridge, and pheasants. But not, necessarily, possums: *"Those that are bagged are usually taken for the fat, which is used as a remedy for a number of ailments, and is claimed to be useful for a great many other things. There are, of course, some people who are very fond of possum meat. These, if they live outside the city, in most cases have a friend who supplies them as a favor free of charge."*

At left is the Neversink Fishing Club House on the George W. Romig Farm in Exeter Township, in 1902. The club formed in 1900, built a one-acre, ten-feet deep fishing dam, stocked it, and built the two-story clubhouse. Membership was limited to 20, and was rapidly filled.

"There are a number of shade trees about the place and it is a very pleasant spot to visit. There are ball and croquet grounds, and it is proposed adding additional attractions next season. There are reading, smoking, and dining rooms, etc., for the use of members. On the second floor, sleeping apartments are provided, and families often spend a few days at a time there."

That's a four feet-eight inches tall girl and a 480-pound black bear hanging next to her. The beauty is Ruth M. Davis, and the beast was shot on a hunting trip in Potter County by Paul B. Davis in 1903. Ruth was the 11-year old daughter of William S. Davis, of Robesonia, and there was no indication if or how she was related to the hunter. According to the accompanying article, it took three shots to bring the bear down.

Mr. Davis was proud of his kill:

"Mr. Davis gave a luncheon to a number of his friends, and bear meat was the leading part of the menu. He sent some of the meat to a number of his friends.

The head and skin will be tanned and made into a rug, which will adorn Mr. Davis' 'den,' at 49 N. 4th Street."

Davis was the assistant city engineer in Reading, and with him on the hunting expedition near Wharton, Pa., was John Halderman of Robesonia.

Get on the Band Wagon....to the Fishin' Hole!

The old band wagon of the Bright Star Cornet Band of Birdsboro was bought by James Kline, proprietor of the Schuylkill Valley House hotel in Monocacy Station in 1898. Kline transformed the 24-passenger wagon into a transport for fishing parties that departed from his hotel.

"Numerous fishing parties leave Monocacy, some living in the old band wagon for a week or more."

Down at the Gum Fort 'Coon and 'Possum Club

About seven miles south of Birdsboro, tucked deep in the woods, was the clubhouse of a very active hunting club that went by the above name. It was founded in 1890 and it is seen here in a 1905 newspaper feature.

"Just why the place was called a fort is not definitely known. Some claim that Lord Cornwallis stopped there over night once upon a time and that a small temporary fort was erected. There is another story which says that many years ago there was a dispute as to the line between two properties on the hill and that one of the contestants erected a fort near a spring surrounded by gum trees. He held his ground for a long time until the matter was settled by the court."

No matter which interesting history rings true, the hunting club evolved from a canvas tent to a two-story frame house built by the members, who included many prominent Berks Countians. The structure included four sleeping rooms, a fireplace built through the funding of Clarence H. Sembower and L.H. Focht, an ice house, and other amenities. Some members retreated to the club for as long as a month, and it was occupied constantly during the hunting seasons. According to the article, the club was reached by taking the W&N Railroad to Cold Run and walking about two miles due east from the station there.

According to one member:

"The place has many tender associations. Here many have come for 15 years for recreation and enjoyment. Away from the rest of the world we can get closer to nature; drink of the cooling waters of the spring in the summer and toast our toes at the open hearth in winter. To leave business and go out there into the forest for a few days gives one a new lease on life and is an experience which only those who have enjoyed it can appreciate."

SECOND - HAND PIANOS
for sale, cheap. Some slightly used. $20 to $100.
ARTHUR WITTICH, - 116 S. SIXTH ST.

Find out what the lowest price is for which a good Carriage or Wagon can be bought by going first to
BIEHL'S, 31 S. 5th St.

When Spitting Was a Crime...

Yellow signs, as seen at right, went up around Reading in the spring of 1902 after a successful drive by the Civic League to have city council pass an Anti-Spitting Ordinance. The first 10x14-inch card was posted on the northwest corner of 5th and Cherry Sts. at the office of Dr. J. Ellis Kurtz.

The city's Anti-Spitting Ordinance included a provision that would impose a fine of from $5 to $50 for anyone caught spitting on any sidewalk anywhere in the city.

"Hardly a day passes that ladies do not have dresses ruined owing to the expectoration on the sidewalks."
 --Reading Eagle, *May 11, 1902*

CAUTION: Spitting or Expectorating on Sidewalks of this City strictly prohibited, under Ordinance approved by the Mayor November 14th, 1901

A New Fountain for People, Horses, and Dogs....

The Women's Christian Temperance Union (W.C.T.U.) was dead-set against the abuse of alcohol in 1903. But, it was all for the drinking of water from the ornate fountain it would build on the northeast corner of Penn Square.

The design and placement of the fountain had to jump through many hoops before its approval by the city and by downtown property owners. The city agreed to supply the water free of charge.

The estimated $750 cost of the fountain would be raised by a public solicitation.

"The design calls for a granite fountain, about ten feet high, four feet wide, and three feet deep.
There will be four pieces–the base, die, carved cap, and a ball surmounting the fountain.
The drinking places for pedestrians will be on the two sides of the die.
The basin for horses (to be large enough for two to drink at one time) will be on the street side of the die.
The trough for dogs will be in the base on the same side.
The drinking parts will be shell-shaped. Scrollwork will lead to the big stone ball on the top. In the cap will be a keystone enclosing the monogram of the Union. The pavement front of the die will be appropriately inscribed, the words to include the name of the W.C.T.U. in full and the date of the erection of the affair."
 --Reading Eagle, *June 14, 1903*

DISASTER!

March 24, 1897: Shortly after midnight, firefighters respond to a spectacular fire on Poplar St. between Elm and Buttonwood Sts. It is the sprawling Acme Bicycle Works, and it is fully involved in flames. A newspaper sketch artist captured the dramatic scene that dominated the front page of the day's news. The entire Reading Fire Department was called by the chief to help fight the blaze, believed to have been started in the enameling room. Due to the large amount of combustible colorings and fluids, the fire spread rapidly. Hundreds of nightshift employees fled the building, and there were no serious injuries. Despite the severity of the fire, the company resumed operations within days.

Physicians' Prescriptions and Family Recipes
CAREFULLY COMPOUNDED AT CUT-RATE PRICES.
BELL'S CUT Rate Drug Store
617 PENN STREET.

Get Some of the Bargains at the
$100,000 FIRE SALE
of the
BRIGHT HARDWARE STOCK
Bright & Company,
504-506 Penn Square, Reading.

Crime...

Whether it was a graphic estimation of the actual crime (right—the 1887 murder of Charles Zabel by his brother, Frank) or a sketch of a robber scurrying through the streets (below, left, the 1895 so-called "white-aproned sharp" or "flying waiter" who robbed a restaurant at 6th and Cherry Sts. in Reading), or a drawing of a crime scene (lower right, John Tomasewski's saloon at 9th and South Sts., which was held up by masked robbers in 1905), *Reading Eagle* sketch artists provided readers with titillating depictions of ne'er-do-wells and the scenes of their crimes.

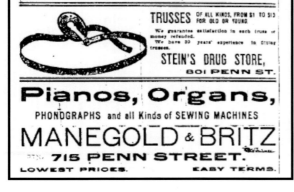

...and Punishment

Berks County's gallows were located in the old county jail, which was in City Park, near 11th and Penn Sts. Depicted at right is the gallows (note the 13 steps) set up for the 1902 execution of 21-year old George Gantz, who was convicted of the murder of 15-year old Annie Etter. The springtime of that year was a busy one on "death row" in Reading.

The picture at lower right shows the cells of Kate Edwards and George Gantz (at the end of the cellblock, with small a small "X" above them. Another condemned prisoner, Samuel Greason, was housed elsewhere in the jail.

Below is a sketch of either Emily Kantner or Reading or Clara Fryburger of Monocacy, who each maintained 12-hour "death watch" shifts at Mrs. Edwards' cell. A convicted murder, Edwards spent her final days with her daughter Alma, who had been born in the prison.

...and more punishment

1903 was a landmark year for Berks County, as it was the year the county got its own scaffold!

The structure was "unveiled" in February of that year after contractor Lloyd Nunnemacher, working at the Merritt Brothers' lumber yard, completed the job.

Made of white pine painted black, the scaffold featured an 8x10 foot deck, trap doors 8 feet, 9 inches from the ground, and a total of 62 parts which made it easy to be dismantled and stored until needed.

The unit was tested in front of workers at the lumber yard and a contingent from the court house.

Shown at left are county commissioners Sanders, Miller, and Johnson, chief clerk Alfred Gunkel, Sheriff Mogel, Board of Prison Inspectors President Joel M. Krick, and others.

The sketch in the middle, left, is the exercise courtyard of the prison. Visible is the brick track, on which prisoners were allowed a 30-minute walk every day. At lower left is what the newspaper described as a "pretty yard," complete with flowers and trees, in another area of the prison. "Few people," the paper noted, "in walking about the reservoir embankment realize that there is a yard of this kind on the other side of the high prison wall."

The sketch below is the corner of the prison in which the gallows were to be erected when necessary.

Even more crime (sort of)...

In a classic sketch (and one of the few of the era that appears to have been signed), the "FLIGHT OF THE FAKIRS" is depicted in the July 21, 1895 *Reading Eagle*. "Night lectures under the glare of flaring torches must cease, according to the orders of the mayor. During the past week, a number of fakirs took a hurried departure from Reading by train and by pike."

Fakirs, Gaycats, and Hobos

Gaycats?
Yes, gaycats.
That was the curious nickname of the ranks of railroad tramps considered to be the worst of all who stole rides on freight trains and kept both municipal and railroad police officers busy.
The "gaycats" were what were described in a 1907 story as "truly troublesome characters." Their sneaky practices were captured in these images.

...and even more punishment (sort of)

OK, you're wondering what a goat has to do with punishment. This goat was Lou Seifert's trusty "watchgoat" at the hotel he operated at Lauer's Garden, 3rd and Walnut Sts., in 1903. "She has a hatred for tramps and suspicious-looking strangers," the newspaper said of her. The feisty nanny goat was known to chase many a prowler or derelict from the premises!

And then, there was "Nellie," the fox terrier who was the constant companion of Reading police officer George Kemp.
"Nellie" was more simply known as "The Cop Dog" as she walked the beat with Officer Kemp along the

riverfront from the Pennsylvania Railroad Station at Penn Street to the Bingaman Street Bridge.
The dog actually belonged to Charles Ziegler, of 514 S. 4th Street, but would—with Mr. Ziegler's consent—leave her yard and go along for the walk.
"Boys on this officer's beat knew well this fox terrier," the *Eagle* story that accompanied this 1904 picture said. "If they are engaged in practices which are not allowed on the highways, the appearance of Nellie is the signal for scattering. With a yell, 'HERE COMES THE COP DOG,' they dash away with the terrier at their heels."
It was noted that on several occasions, Nellie discovered intoxicated men sleeping along the river front, some of which were said to have been perilously close to roll into the canal or river.
With a loud barking fit, Nellie would alert Officer Kemp to their presence, and the two would save the poor soul from what could have been a horrible fate.
Nellie was also known for some very clever tricks, including turning back flips!

Inside City Hall, 1903

That's Reading Mayor Edward Yeager in his office in City Hall in 1903. And, quite an office it was!

"The walls and ceiling are covered with a paper of rich pattern with Persian and Turkish effects. The red and white border is especially pretty. The chandelier has 12 burners and there are fixtures for both gas and electricity. The floor is covered with a velvet carpet into which the foot sinks in walking over it."

The office was adorned with oak furniture, a ship miniature made by an "inmate of the county home," a typewriter desk for the mayor's secretary, E.L. Lindenmuth, and talking tubes that were connected with offices on other floors of the hall.

"It is an office such as few Pennsylvania mayors have in respect to furnishing and good taste."

One thing the mayor had that few, if any, other mayors had was a mounted horned toad...given by friend Joseph O'Reilly.

• • •

At left, Registry Clerk Caleb Weidner, seen at his desk on the third floor of City Hall.

Above, Mayor Gerber presides over Police Court in the northeast corner of the basement of City Hall. He is seated at left, while Police Chief Richard M. Whitman is seated to his left. That's a Reading police officer standing at left and an "offender" to the right

"From four to sixteen prisoners have been arraigned before him daily. The most common charge is drunkenness. Very few of the offenders get off without punishment. The fine, as a rule, was $3, $1.25 costs, or 48 hours. Not one-third were able to pay and they stood committed."

The mayor was a no-nonsense, but fair adjudicator.

"If the allegations are not serious, the case is promptly disposed of. If the offense is more than ordinary, the accused, in pointed words, is impressed with the folly of his actions and conduct and punished accordingly. He is cautioned not to repeat the misbehavior or the sentence would be much more severe if brought in again."

In May, 1904, the city's Engineering Office moved into new quarters in City Hall, and its suite of offices were among the finest in the building. At right is a view of the meeting room of the Board of Public Works.

"A rich pattern of embossed paper covers the walls. On the floor is a beautiful black and red velvet carpet. A large oak table handsomely carved occupies the center of the room, and around it are seven revolving oak chairs of unique design. it has all the conveniences including talking tubes, telephones communicating with other departments, etc."

A Hobo, a Hard Worker, and a <u>Very</u> Large Chocolate Rabbit!

Yes, that's right...it's a chocolate rabbit that youngster is riding. It's a one-ton solid chocolate rabbit, no less!

"It is considered the finest piece of work of its kind ever produced in the United States."

The gargantuan confection was made by Herman Schober, an employee at Luden's in 1905.

"Should this rabbit be made into five and ten-cent chocolate cakes, and these laid side-by-side, they would make a row reaching two miles."

The big bunny was put on display on the second floor of the Dives, Pomeroy & Stewart store for all to see.

At lower left is Francis Bergman, a roadside vagrant who caught the attention of a Reading Eagle reporter who believed he had a story or two to tell. And, he did.

"Why am I a tramp? Well, I became a tramp when I was out of work and had practically nothing else to do, and later I remained a vagrant because I did not care to do anything else."

Mr. Bergman came to Berks County from Germany in 1869 but found it hard to find work.

"Am I disappointed with my life? No. I have no cares. While I have not done the world any good, neither have I ever wronged man, woman, or child."

On the other end of the scale was John Hahn, of Lorane. Interviewed at age 75, Mr. Hahn boasted that he had hardly missed a day of work in his life. Hahn worked in iron mills, the railroad, a farm, and at the time of the interview (1905), Seidel's Forge, near Lorane, in Exeter Township.

"Mr. Hahn is six feet tall, of splendid physical proportions, and says he is sound as a dollar."

City Streetscapes...circa 1903

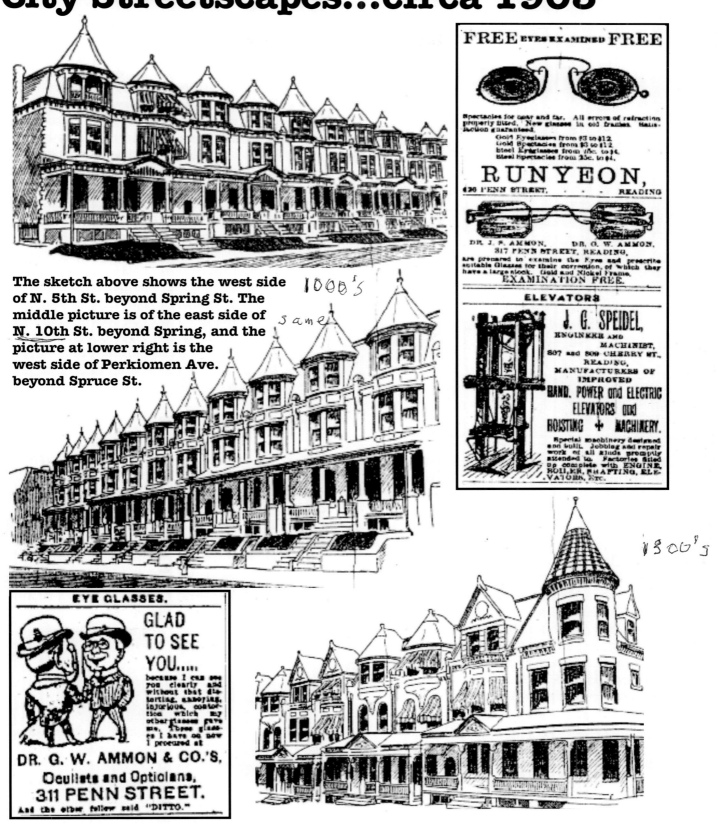

The sketch above shows the west side of N. 5th St. beyond Spring St. The middle picture is of the east side of N. 10th St. beyond Spring, and the picture at lower right is the west side of Perkiomen Ave. beyond Spruce St.

Keeping the streets clean...

...White Wings and Wrathful Women...

What started in New York City spread to Reading in 1907 as troops of "White Wings" took to the streets to keep Reading clean and tidy. The so-called "White Wings" were the brainchild of Col. George E. Waring, who was given charge by New York's Tammany Hall to clean that city's streets of mounds of litter and filth. He dressed his street cleaners in white and gave them the catchy name.

It was flamboyant city entrepreneur William Abbott Witman who introduced the "White Wings" concept to Reading when he was granted the street-cleaning contract by the city. About 20 men dressed in what were called white "duck suits" and caps as they patrolled the streets with brooms, brushes, shovels, and wheelbarrows.

Not only city crews were at work keeping Reading's streets clean. Dedicated–and a bit angry–bands of neighborhood women (and sometimes men) pitched in as well.

In the 1902 drawing to the right, a group of women who lived on Jefferson Street below Schuylkill Avenue, are seen doing their volunteer work.

It was recorded that Kate Rickenbach, Loretta Rickenbach, Esther Fertig, Mary Wunderly, Martha DeTemple, and others were among the Jefferson Street women who took matters (and brooms) in their own hands and kept the cobblestone streets, and concrete sidewalks clean.

"For over a year past, not a bit of work, or any attempt to do so, has been made by the city on our square, so we had to do the work ourselves. As we live not in the heart of the city, they don't seem to care how our street looks."
--Kate Rickenbach

Flavored Soda Water... A Penny a Glass

Shoppers and workers in downtown Reading could refresh themselves in the hot summer of 1903 at any number of street vendors. Soda water available in a half-dozen flavors was the best-seller. A small glass, a penny—a large glass, two pennies. The vendors also sold orangeade, pretzels, and peanuts.

John Tognetti's portable soda fountain, northeast corner of 7th and Penn.

Haraly Anasoparlys' orangeade stand, near 5th and Penn Sts.

John Duros at his orangeade stand on Penn St. near 6th.

...and waffles, too!

While folks were slaking their thirst with a cool glass of orangeade or sarsaparilla, they could also avail themselves of the two "waffle wagons" that roamed the streets of town in 1904. The waffle vendors mapped out routes through Reading and folks would look forward to their arrival around dinnertime when they could get the waffles "hot off the iron."

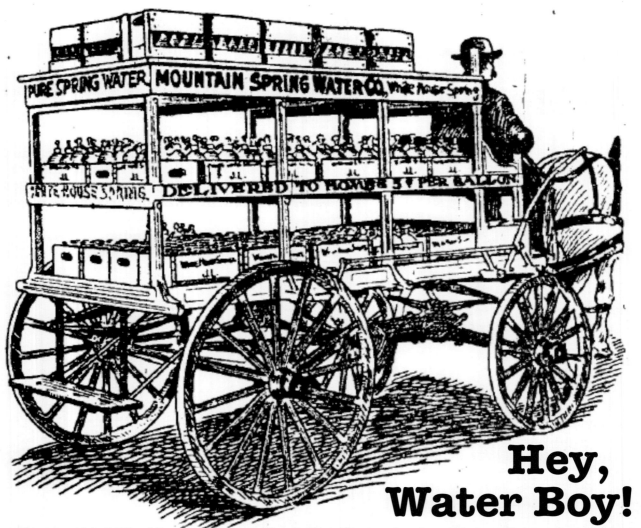

Hey, Water Boy!

So, you think the idea of home-delivered spring water is a 21st century convenience. Well, think again.

As seen in this 1904 depiction, the Mountain Spring Water Company was one of several bottled water firms that provided alternative drinking and cooking water to residents in Reading. At the time, the city's reservoir water supply was under attack by many who claimed its smell and taste were less than optimum. Especially in summer months, carts filled with spring water made their deliveries in Reading and surrounding cities. The Mountain Spring Water Company obtained its water from the White House Spring on Neversink Mountain.

"A tunnel 250 feet long reaches the spot where this sparkling water, filtered by nature, percolates through sand and rocks. It is so deep in the side of the mountain that it cannot be contaminated with impurities."

--*Reading Eagle*

It was said that the company used the water to also bottle soda, seltzer, birch beer, and other drinks. According to its proprietors, John and Edward Lawrence, 75 gallons an hour could be tapped from the source.

What did a gallon of fresh, mountain spring water cost in 1904?
Remember....a *gallon?*
Five cents.

Water... ...Water

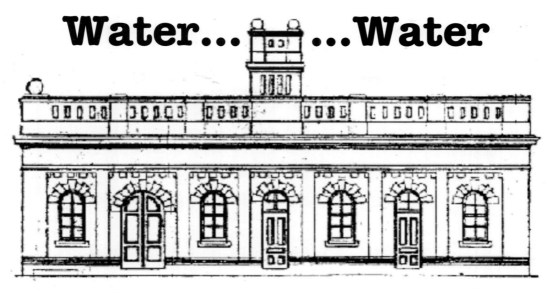

The City of Reading's water supply system was as "high-tech" as it could get in 1908, when construction of the Maidencreek Filter Plant began.

"As to the method of operation, the water will be taken from the Maiden Creek and allowed to flow through a five-foot concrete conduit to the filters. After being filtered thoroughly, it will be carried by a 36-inch cast iron pipe to a small suction well east of the pumping station. From the well it will be dumped to the Hampden Reservoir and distributed...."

The Maidencreek facility was being built at the same time the Bernhart's Dam reservoir was being completed. The new filter house was to be built of pearl brick with granite trimmings. The total cost of the filtering plant was $182,885. It, and the Bernhart's Dam project were paid for through a half-million dollar loan for water improvements authorized by the voters in 1907.

The Egelman Dam filtration plant (above) went into service in 1903. It was a designed as a simple, "slow sand" filtration plant that could filter about 350,000 gallons a day.

In 1905, the city of Reading opened its new "slow sand method" water filtration plant just outside the city limits at 20th St. and Perkiomen Ave. in Mt. Penn. The entire project, land and filtering system, cost a whopping $100,000. Water in the 101-million gallon Antietam Lake reservoir was purified at the filtration plant before it was sent into the water pipes in the city below. The two structures on the grounds were an "inlet regulator house" and a "gate house." At right are pictures of the portable sand washer that was used to cleanse the sand through which the water flowed before it entered the city's water system.

Seen in the 1906 view at left is the 42-million gallon Bernhart's reservoir in Muhlenberg Township. Even then, the lake gave the city water bureau its share of challenges.

"The Bernhart, like all other unfiltered reservoirs used for domestic purposes, has given annoyances from time to time because of bad taste and odor."

To remedy that, the city voted to equip Bernhart's with a filtration system as soon as funds were available.

Rare views into the lifestyle of the toll-taker of a Berks County covered bridge are revealed in these views of the Stoudt's Ferry Bridge in Muhlenberg Township. The bridge is seen above, while the lower photo shows the crude box in which the "bridgeman" slept. According to a 1905 article in the *Eagle*, the bridge marked the spot where the Schuylkill Canal towpath crossed from the east to the west bank of the river. In its prime, about 2,000 boats came down the canal. The bridgeman collected the toll (five cents per horse, one cent per human) from the boat team driver. If the driver had no money, the bridgekeeper would lower a small box down to the canal boat captain, who would pay the toll.

There was a sort of early "E-Z Pass" arrangement for frequent foot passengers who could pay a flat 25-cent seasonal toll in advance. Farmers would be assessed from $2.50 to $600 a year for their use of the bridge.

On June 9, 1890, the tolls were eliminated.

The bridgeman's job was not done with the cessation of toll-taking. He was also responsible for maintaining the bridge and tending various items and supplies that were stored there by the county, which owned the span.

The Stoudt's Ferry Bridge "bridgeman" in the late 19th century was responsible for the upkeep of the bridge and its approaches. To that end, a closet, planing bench, and a full set of tools was supplied by the county.

The keeper's tiny hutch, in which he slept, was sparse. He slept on a mattress placed on a board, under which was space for his watchdog. He lived there rent-free, and was paid $30 a month.

The county stored coal, wood, and corn cobs in sheds and piles around the bridge. It was the keeper's job to guard that storage area, as well. And, although he closed the gates at dark, he would be awakened should anyone choose to make a night crossing of the bridge.

In the newspaper account of the bridgeman's responsibilities, it was noted that past tolltakers at Stoudt's Ferry included Christian Eddinger, David Biery, John Binckley, Harry Wagner, Jacob Strause, Joe Steffy, James Kauffman, and Charles Peiffer.

The bridgeman at the time of the writing was Cyrus Roth. Mr. Roth told the reporter that on warm evenings he would frequently lie down in the cool bridge. But, as the night went on and temperatures dropped, he would retreat to his little shed.

Down Goes the Old...

...Up Rises the New

That was the plan for the southwest corner in 1905 when it was announced that "The Fashion," a store located at 518 Penn Street, would relocate into a new, Colonial-style building at the southwest corner of Penn Square.

The top picture shows what was located there at the time, and the picture at right is the architect's rendering of the proposed new building.

The Fashion was owned by W.H. Bash, and was a popular store that sold furs, notions, millinery, and other items. While the new building was under construction and The Fashion's 518 Penn store was vacated to make room for Keller's China Store, The Fashion set up temporary quarters at 413-415 Penn Street.

"The proposed new building," the *Reading Eagle* proclaimed, "will be one of the most modern and attractive along the thoroughfare."

A funny thing happened as the old buildings were torn down in preparation for construction. For that, see the next page.

Will Work for Wood.....

When the buildings were being torn down on the southwest corner of Penn Square in April, 1905, a group of neighborhood children made the most of the demolition. Contractor D. Elmer Dampman had actually taken out an ad in the *Reading Eagle* to inform any and all citizens that as the structures went down, the scrap wood would be available, free.

Kids brought their wagons to stock up on what would be kindling, firewood, or—who knows—framework for a tree house!

Mr. Dampman became quite popular with the scavengers. "I'd vote for Dampman for mayor or any other office," one young man was quoted. "Say, this is a cinch. The wood you want, don't cost anything to take it away, and it comes so easy."

It's a Bird! It's a Plane! No...it's a Sweet Potato!

Sometimes, the strangest things made the papers back in 1903. Take, for example, this "Odd-Shaped Sweet Potato," as the headline heralded it. The curious spud was found in M.L. Hafer's Market at 11th and Muhlenberg Sts.

What's not quite clear in the picture is the neck of the yam-bird, which is a small ham bone. The bone was in the soil, and the potato vine grew through it, creating the strange shape. The "legs" were added by Mr. Hafer.

School Days, School Days...

The "Mt. Sunset School House," Heidelberg Township, ca. 1900.

WYOMISSING, 1907: Built on Belmont Ave. to accommodate the 150 students who lived in West Reading, this building included four classrooms and something new—two playrooms.

"Wyomissing is the first borough in the county to take this advanced step and is ahead of Reading in this line."
       --Reading Eagle, *1907*

LONGSWAMP TOWNSHIP, 1905: The new Longswamp High School building (right), on a hill about a half-mile from Shamrock, afforded a wonderful view of the surrounding countryside and included four classrooms, a library, and a directors' meeting room. Also in the plans for the building were provisions for a total of 67 feet of blackboards.

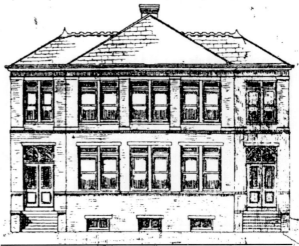

SHILLINGTON, 1901: At left is the four-room schoolhouse that replaced the two-room schoolhouse in the borough. The builder was James Matz, who modeled the building after the Park School (Perkiomen Ave. and Franklin St.) in Reading. The members of the Cumru Township school board said it would be one of the finest buildings in the county outside of the city, and as well-equipped as any school, even in Reading.

A Landmark Year for Mt. Penn Landmarks

"...it renders it especially desirable as a place for home-building. Protected against the winds of winter and not subject to excessive heat of summer, the temperature in the borough usually ranges about five degrees cooler in summer and about the same number of degrees warmer in winter than in Reading at the same hour."

The *Reading Eagle* story was referring to the burgeoning borough of Mt. Penn in its May 20, 1906 edition that heralded the many attributes and improvements.

The article noted that a full half of the buildings in the borough in 1906 were built in 1905–and because of favorable property prices, the borough was sure to grow from its population of about 300.

"There is quite a demand for real estate here. There is not at this time an empty house in the borough and houses can be rented faster than they can be built."

The town at the time boasted a flour and feed store, a coal and lumber yard, a blacksmith shop, two wagon factories, a cigar maker, two grocery stores, two ice houses, a rug factory, a pipe organ factory, a flour sack factory, a post office (upper left), two hotels, a school house (left), and two churches, including Faith Lutheran, which is seen below.

"That the borough of Mt. Penn enjoys a high credit is shown by the widespread inquiry for the new bonds. Bankers in Chicago, Toledo, Cleveland, Buffalo, New York, Philadelphia, and other cities are keeping closely in touch with the borough authorities."

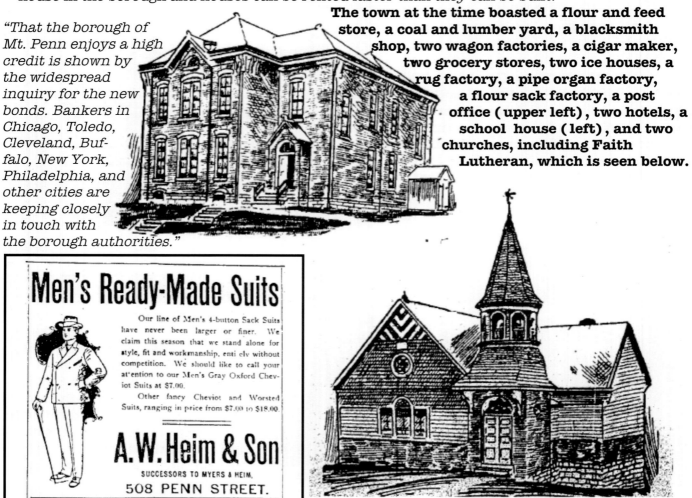

Here We Grow!

Note the sign imprinted on the front of the trolley– "ONLY 5c FARE TO ROSEDALE ADDITION." That was one of the lure for "city folk" to hop the streetcar and have a look at the new suburb north of town. Promotional advertising promised sparkling water, shade trees, and properties that will "double and redouble in value"

1913

1913

61

Glenside For Sale: Cheap!

"Glenside lots are correct. There are no poor ones." That was the message in a series of ads in 1905 that touched off a land rush to the city's newest suburb, Glenside. Lots went for $63-136 apiece during the sale. Cash customers got a ten percent discount. Installment payments of 50 cents to a dollar a week could be arranged. The neighborhood's proximity to the city, just across the Schuylkill Avenue Bridge (below) was one of it's biggest drawing cards.

"It is the premier home location. It has natural drainage, insuring healthful and cleanly conditions, in addition to giving a magnificent and unbroken view of the surrounding country."

Going Downtown

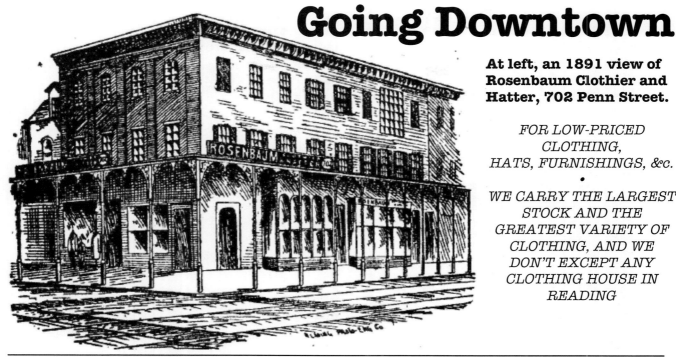

At left, an 1891 view of Rosenbaum Clothier and Hatter, 702 Penn Street.

FOR LOW-PRICED CLOTHING, HATS, FURNISHINGS, &c.

•

WE CARRY THE LARGEST STOCK AND THE GREATEST VARIETY OF CLOTHING, AND WE DON'T EXCEPT ANY CLOTHING HOUSE IN READING

At right, "The Big New Furniture Store," H.J. Gring & Co., at 19-23 S. 4th Street. ca. 1902

H.J. GRING HAS GOTTEN TO BE A POWERFUL FACTOR IN THE FURNITURE BUSINESS OF READING BECAUSE OF ITS INEXPENSIVE LOCATION EQUIVALENT TO THE SAVING ON AN INVESTMENT OF THOUSANDS OF DOLLARS, WHEREBY IT CAN AND ACTUALLY DOES SELL AT LOWER PRICES THAN OTHER STORES

At left, the "new double front store of C.K. Whitner & Co., Penn Square, in 1899.

THE ENTIRE STORE IS ONE OF THE MOST COMPLETE OF ITS KIND IN PENN'A.

Long before there were suburban "power centers" filled with busy retail establishments there was Penn Square in downtown Reading. Seen below, left, is the Gately & Britton store that stood at 940 Penn Street for many years. At right is a depiction of what had become The G.M. Britton Co. by 1905. The store had also expanded greatly and moved to the 400 block of Penn Street.

"Our new home. A busy block surely, full of life, full of hustle. We have pictured it for you [below]. *It extends from Fourth to Fifth Streets on the south side of Penn Square. You will notice our store, the third one from the right. Our new store extends from Penn Square to Cherry Street and consists of four floors and a basement. It is filled with bright, new goods. Old friends are here and you are made to feel at home."*

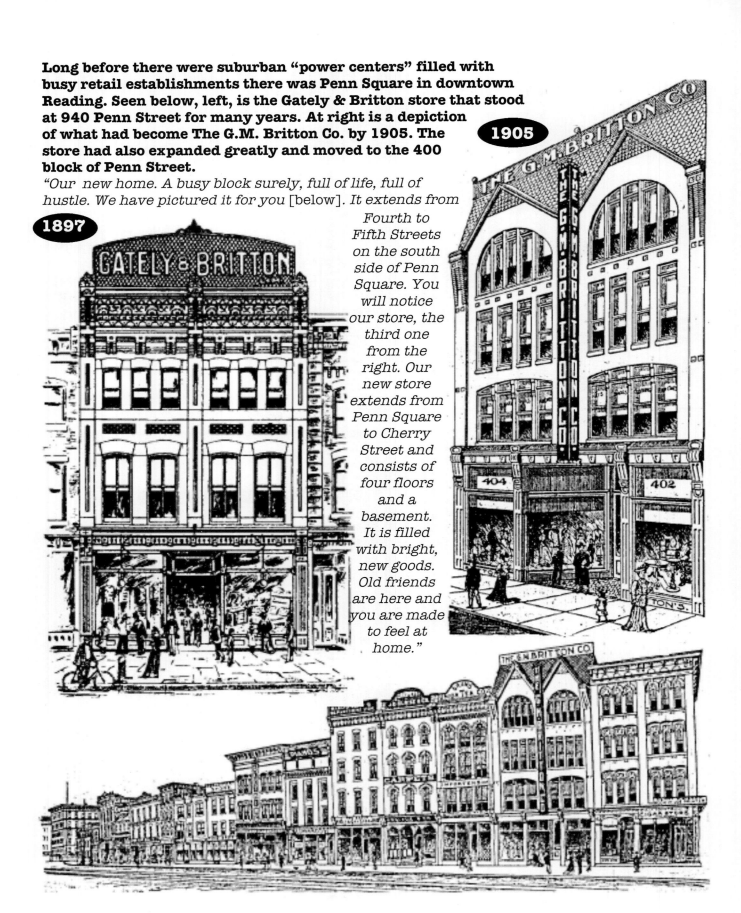

After This...

The headline for the story that accompanied the illustration at left in a 1901 newspaper read:

WORKING AT A DIZZY HEIGHT AT 5th AND PENN

Reading's first real "skyscraper," the Colonial Trust Company building, was rising higher day by day to the delight of downtown workers and shoppers who followed progress of its construction every day.

"People watch with great interest the work of the riggers who nimbly skip about the top. They work at this dizzy height apparently unconscious of danger."

...There Was This

Of course, downtown workers and shoppers may still see the result of the nimble riggers' work. The nine-story, 119-room building was opened in 1903.

"It is built of hydraulic pressed brick, Roman size, and laid in mortar to match the color. The halls, corridors, etc., are laid with trazza, which is a mixture of chopped marble and cement. All the stairways are marble tread. There are toilet rooms on every floor. Of course, the handsomest quarters in the building are those to be occupied by the bank on the first floor."

OK, About That "First Skyscraper" Thing...

Calling the Colonial Trust Company building "Reading's First Skyscraper" could have been debated if the six-story "Baer Building" at Church and Court Sts. could be considered a "skyscraper." It was constructed in 1900, three years before the Colonial Trust structure.

It was certainly a modern marvel when it rose next to George F. Baer's office building on Washington Street, where the Reading Iron Company and Baer, Snyder & Zieber had their offices. Seen below from the Church Street aspect (left) and from Court Street, the building was built with Indiana limestone for the first two stories and mottled brick and terra cotta the rest of the way up. There were 70 offices built into the structure, which cost $75,000 to erect.

"It will make a solid block on Church Street, and the Post Office yard will allow an excellent view of it from Washington Street. It will be an ornament to that part of the city."

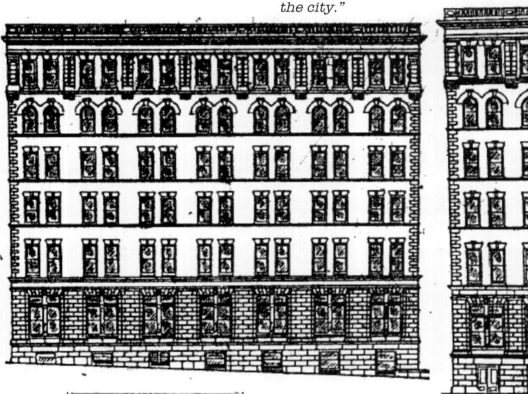

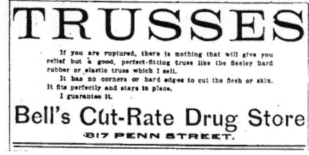

Penn Street in 1895 was considerably more crowded with carriages, streetcars, and people than it is today. Look closely at the sketch below and note the backup of hundreds of people (under the canopy), streetcars, and other vehicles as a train rumbles through the 7th and Penn Sts. crossing.

According to an article in the November 3, 1895 newspaper, "The blockades are becoming more frequent of late and there is much complaint made by citizens who are detained there on account of passing trains. Many think that the railroad should make some arrangement by which all coal and freight trains could be taken around the city. This is a nuisance. The businessmen in the vicinity are considerably annoyed by reason of the large crowds standing in front of their places of business and blocking the way to their stores. After the trains have cleared the way there is a regular blockade and the scenes in that neighborhood resemble those seen on Broadway, New York!"

Although passenger trains moved swiftly through the intersection, the long and slow coal trains caused the longest and most frustrating delays.

There were remedies suggested, however, as are depicted on page 69.

Charles Breneiser, a tobacconist at 7th and Penn Street, made a prediction in 1895: "The running of trains around the city is bound to come sooner or later. The Reading Company, I am informed, has secured the right of way on the western side of the river, and the time will come when all coal and freight trains will run via that section."

Going Down...

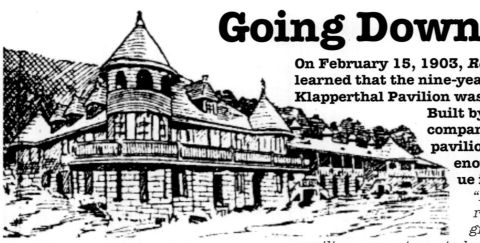

On February 15, 1903, *Reading Eagle* readers learned that the nine-year old Klapperthal Pavilion was to be demolished. Built by the Reading Railway company, the entertainment pavilion failed to attract enough patrons to continue in operation.

"It has often been remarked that it was a great pity that the big pavilion was not erected on top of Neversink."

...Going Up

The new (1903) "monster" United Gas & Improvement gas holder at the foot of S. 5th St. stood 107 feet tall and held 504,000 feet of natural gas.

New Bijou Theatre
WEEK BEGINNING MONDAY, MATINEE, OCT. 30

Matinees Monday, Thursday and Saturday
J. HERBERT MACK'S

WORLD BEATERS BURLESQUERS CO.

CELEBRATED CHORUS OF STUNNING SHOW GIRLS GORGEOUSLY GOWNED

The Performance Starts With an Automobile Chorus as an Opening Wedge for the Funny Farce Comedy,

Jolly Old Sports

And is Highly Seasoned With Riotous Revelry and Rollicking Music.

The Biggest ALL-STAR OLIO
of Clean Cut Vaudeville Ever Presented, Headed With

1--MAY GEBHARDT--1
and Her 20 YANKEE DOODLE GIRLS.
2--MAJOR CASPER NOWAK--2
The Smallest Comedian in the World.
3--BOHANNON and COREY--3
Will Introduce Their Illuminated Grotto, Together With Song Illustrations.
4--Quigg, Edwards & Nickerson--4
Comedy Musical Trio, Introducing Mr. Nickerson, America's Greatest Cornet Soloist.
5--SISTERS DeFOREST--5
Catchy Songs and Artistic Dancing.
6--McFarland and McDonald--6
The Laughsmiths.
7--NIBLO and SPENCER--7
Artistic Dancing Exercises.
8--THE MACKER SCOPE--8
Scenes from Life.

And as a Fitting Conclusion, for Want of a Better Name, We Call Our Finisher

=====ALL AT SEA=====

This is the Spectacular Portion of the Show—Electric Effects, Gaudy Gowns, Dazzling Scenery Beyond Comparison, and 25 DASHING SHOW GIRLS and TALENTED CHORUSTERS.
The Prices for This Big Show Will Remain the Same as Usual.
Evening—10c, 15c, 25c and 50c.
Matinees—10c, 20c and 30c. First Five Rows, 50c.

COMING WEEK, NOV. 6, M. M. THEISE'S
WINE, WOMEN AND SONG

Dreams and Schemes...

Sometimes, things just don't work out as some had hoped. Take, for example, this idea to eliminate the growing traffic congestion situation at the 7th and Penn Sts. railroad crossing in 1894.

The Davis Brothers engineering firm of Reading proposed two identical pedestrian footbridges that would loop up and over the railroad tracks–one north of Penn Street and one south of the street. Thirty-two steps would lead to ornamental iron decks 20 feet over the tracks. The bridges would be 35 feet long.

The engineers claimed that between 200 and 300 pedestrians could cross in a minute's time.

And then, there was that plan for pedestrian tunnels under 7th St.

Yes, a plan for two matching pedestrian tunnels on the north and the south sides of Penn Street, under the 7th Street railroad tracks. The tunnels would take pedestrians about ten feet under the tracks. The idea was a favorable alternative to the bridge, according to the *Eagle*, "because the overhead bridge is objectionable for ladies in stormy weather." There were actually several other plans submitted for the elimination of the crossing. One other called for a full-blown vehicular tunnel under the railroad tracks (below); another proposed the elevation of the railroad tracks by 8.2 feet up and over not only Penn Street, but as a viaduct also over Franklin and Chestnut Streets.

The Old....

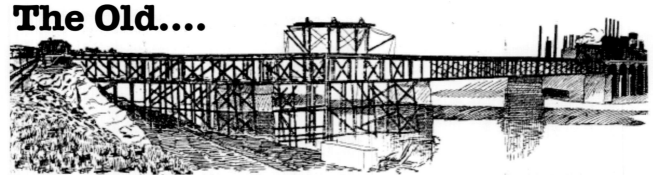

The picture above shows the Reading Railroad's bridge over the Schuylkill River in 1902, as it was being rebuilt to accommodate heavier train traffic. The busy Lebanon Valley Branch maintained limited traffic on the bridge as it was bolstered and widened. The bridge replaced an earlier structure (whose pillars still stand) which was destroyed by a fire during the railroad strike riots of 1877.

...The New

The new bridge that carried the Lebanon Valley Branch of the Reading Railroad over the Schuylkill was erected by the Phoenix Iron Company, and stretched 626 feet across and 80 feet over the river.

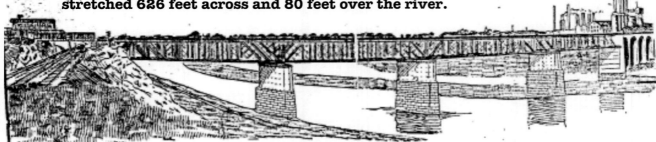

Takin' Care of Business...

Directors of the Reading Clearing House Association are pictured in the firm's board room in 1904. The RCHA was an organization of local banks, managed by Reading National Bank. Its members met every morning to coordinate the financial needs of each bank in the city.

In 1901, Reading boasted 13 independent banks. The front doors of ten of them are pictured here. Top row, from left: National Union Bank, Farmers' National Bank, Second National Bank, Keystone National Bank, Reading Trust Co. Bottom row, from left: Reading National Bank, Penn National Bank, Pennsylvania Trust Co., Berks County Trust Co., Citizens' Bank. Others included First National Bank, Colonial Trust Co., and Schuylkill Valley Bank.

Making Stoves....

Stove making was big business in Reading beginning in about 1860, and by 1906 there were three large factories that produced about 45,000 stoves, heaters, and ranges every year. An article that accompanied the above sketches of the stove making process said the industry started when John R. Painter, Jesse Orr, P.W. Nagle, Elijah Bull, William H. Shick, Henry C. Posey, William Grander and Jasper Sheeler formed a partnership to start the first plant. The largest company in the city in 1906 was the Reading Stove Works, and the Mt. Penn Stove Works (which was in the city) wasn't far behind.

"Go where you will, you will be apt to find Reading-made stoves on sale. they have gained a worldwide reputation, and for completeness in every detail they cannot be excelled."

...and Baking Loaves

Another "hot" venture in Reading in 1906 was the baking of bread. There were 52 bakeries in the city that year, when bread sold for a nickel a loaf. The sketches seen here depicted baking at Henry Schofer's Sons, 229 N. 8th Street. They show the dough-mixer (left), the dough-weigher (lower left), and the loaf forming machine.

"They Employ Several Thousands, Mostly Girls."

Without argument, one of the biggest industries in the area around the turn of the century was the manufacturing of hosiery. In 1906, more than 30 knitting mills could be found in and around Reading and most, as the headline above noted, were staffed almost entirely by young women. Below is an actual quote from the *Reading Eagle* story that accompanied these random pictures of the looping, topping, and knitting departments of a city knitting mill.

"They are not wives and mothers, not yet. That most of them will ultimately become so is significantly indicated by the youthfulness of all found at the trade and also, it is proved by statistics. Knitting in its most modern manifestation, then, is still the woman's trade, more so than clerical work, of shop selling, or typewriting, more than in the old days, for instead of coming to her after marriage it helps her to get married."

Cigar Making: The People...

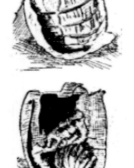

...and the Places

Around the turn of the 20th century, when you smoked a cigar, there was a very good chance that the "stogie" may have been manufactured in one of Reading's 200 cigar factories. The industry, which started in town in the mid-19th century, was booming in 1906, when an estimated 160 million cigars were produced by the thousands who were employed in the trade. Among the largest producers were, bottom pictures from left, J.L. & M.F. Greene Leaf Tobacco Co., 21 S. 6th St.; Julius G. Hansen's Cigar Factory, 10th and Spring Sts.; and the Charles Maerz plant 10th and Cherry Sts.

Among the brands of cigars manufactured in Reading:
• Civil Rights • Sunny Clime • Mystic Star • Fair Weight • Juniata • Cuban Federation • Our Leader • Our Pusher • Alpaca • Pot-sto • Racer • My Jack • O-We-Go • Bloma de Cuba • Pedro de Florez • Royal Windsor • Y-B • Lady Berks • Pompy

In 1906, the average cigar factory worker earned from $7 to $16 a week, depending on their skill. Most Reading-made cigars sold for between five and ten cents apiece.

An Industry to Dye For...

The Prospect Dye Works, 1122 to 1132 Moss Street in Reading, was among the industries that was spawned by the abundance of knitting mills in and around the city. Opened in 1899, the firm took in yarn, hosiery, underwear, piece goods, and other knitted and woven fabrics, and gave them their colors. The dye works complex was made up of the main building (above, right), and the printing department, which was located in four former rowhomes (above, left), which were gutted and connected to the main building.

"Everything is done by machinery through scientific methods. Hosiery dyed with their process has a fast black color, which is perfectly harmless to the wearer, and the dyeing has not deteriorated the quality of the goods."

In the sketches below are scenes in several of the departments at the Prospect Dye Works. Clockwise from top left: A view of the dye house, a portion of the saturating room for "fast black" dyeing of hosiery, the shipping room, and the engine room.

"The process of dyeing fast black is a good illustration of what science has accomplished in the industrial world."

Gettin' the Paper Out...

13-year old Harry Killian, his 12-year old sister, Minnie, and their dog "Nellie" are pictured here on their *Reading Eagle* delivery route in Reamstown in 1905. The papers would be stacked in the wagon after they were delivered by trolley to the town.

"The dog draws the wagon while his young master walks and distributes the papers. The dog is well trained to either wagon or sled. When all the papers are delivered, young Killian occupies the seat in the express wagon and drives home. Nellie usually receives a bone after finishing her route."

That's an unidentified *Reading Eagle* newsboy standing near the lamp post at 3rd and Penn Streets and his kid sister hawking a paper to a businessman in 1904. In a brief interview with a reporter, the lad disclosed that "sis" started helping him with his paper sales when he came down with a case of measles, and has assisted him ever since.

"Since the commencement of the war between Japan and Russia, the number of boys engaged in the sale of newspapers has greatly increased. The majority attend school during the day, and as soon as the afternoon session is concluded, they flock to the newspaper offices to lay in a supply."

During a United Traction Co. strike in January, 1901, the papers were delivered by *Eagle* "canvassers" who used the latest transportation technology. At right are *Eagle* delivery man Thomas Kline and driver Harry Burhans behind the stick of a Duryea Power Co. car.

(CONTINUED ON NEXT PAGE)

The *Reading Eagle's* new "web perfecting press," 1890

(CONTINUED FROM PREVIOUS PAGE)
Kline and Burhans left Reading at 4 p.m. on a route that would deliver bundles of papers agents who would then distribute them to 1,000 readers between the city and Womelsdorf.

"By the time they reached Springmont the occupants were covered from head to foot with mud and water. The bundle was dropped off and then they were off for Sinking Spring.

It was found that owing to the terrible condition of the road that it was not the most favorable for that kind of motive power."

All along their route, which took them into the darkness of night, eager readers awaited their arrival.

"When they reached Sinking Spring, the people who had congregated showed their appreciation of the enterprise and gave the plucky men a hearty sendoff.

The next stop was Wernersville. Here there was another delegation of Eagle readers and when the auto was guided up to the hotel someone cried, 'You can't get ahead of the Eagle!'"

There were times when the men doubted they would make the perilous journey.

"On several occasions it was thought that the machine would collapse, but it didn't, and Robesonia was passed on time. Then came the final tug and the run to Womelsdorf was made without much difficulty."

The telephone department of the *Eagle* on duty on election night, 1896

77

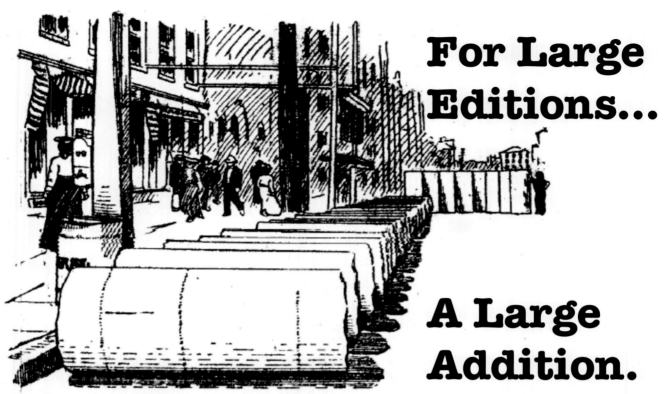

For Large Editions...

A Large Addition.

Seen above are some of the 40 rolls of newsprint that were unloaded about every 20 days on the Penn Street side of the *Reading Eagle* offices at 6th and Penn Streets in the early 1900s. This 1903 view served to illustrate an article that explained how much each roll weighed (1,200 pounds) and how long the rolls would be if one carload (40 rolls) would be extended from end-to-end. The story graphically explained that by claiming that the paper would open up to more than 143 miles. Furthermore, the paper in those 40 rolls would cover every paved street in Reading, and every park in the city.

At right is a sketch of the unusual expansion of the *Eagle* building annex on the S. 6th Street side. The building's 225-ton roof was lifted to accommodate the construction of two additional floors that would house the press rooms, carriers' rooms, collector's office, composing, and job printing rooms of the newspaper. The roof was jacked up while the building was expanded beneath it. It was then lowered when the structure was completed.

Once Upon a Time In Berks County

ANNOTATIONS BY

GEORGE M. MEISER IX

President of the Historical Society of Berks County

THE NUMBERS OF THE NOTES CORRESPOND WITH NUMBERS OF THE PREVIOUS PAGES

1– The Wanner Building., long used as a printing establishment (the *New Era* was printed there) and removed when Court St. was widened, was erected by wealthy and successful attorney Peter D. Wanner whose mansion at 14th and Walnut could be seen from most parts of Reading for years. Wanner committed suicide in 1912.

2– 2nd National Bank Building, off the S.E. corner of 3rd and Penn, is now part of Gilbert's Furniture; its handsome brownstone façade covered over.
The Lerch and Bright Building, on the diamond on the S.E. corner of 5th and Penn, was once a major Reading hardware emporium.
In 1896, Mr. Umble more than doubled the size of the original Mansion House hotel; two stories of brick added above the original four-story brownstone building. He added southward to a height of six stories. It was razed in 1937.

3– The Pennsy frame depot, which sat immediately north of the iron-truss Penn Street Bridge, was a temporary facility. Its ornate Victorian replacement followed soon after this view was taken.

4– Watch boxes existed at every point where tracks crossed major thoroughfares, in the city and in the county. In the 1940's, old fellows used to congregate at the one at 7th and Penn, sitting around on the curb and chatting for hours each day.

6– The Atlantic Refining Co. had its original headquarters at Giles' Lock, Reading, at the south side of the Lebanon Valley R.R. Bridge, just east of the tracks. Old photos show a large office building and huge tanks there. Early deliveries were made using horse-drawn tank-wagons.
Oley Valley cars ran to Boyertown until July 1932.

7- The coming of dependable automatic signals and switching devices made obsolete the once familiar high observation towers to facilitate visual judgments and control regulation. This feature coincided with opening of the Belt Line, built to route traffic away from center-city Reading.

8- The greatest local activity along the river, including the River Carnivals of the 1890's, took place at Hain's Lock-on land now owned by Carpenter Technology.

9- A number of vintage houseboats, constructed on discarded coal scowls, survived until the Depression, at which time nearly all were dismantled for firewood-and not always by their owners.

10- The "Atlantic" was renamed the "Carrie." It and "Rosa" were disassembled by C. Howard Hiester and incorporated in a double-home built at 116 Park Ave. in the 18th Ward, for many years the residence of Howard and his uncle.

11- Mountain Spring Assn. ceased operations in late 2005. The property was sold in March, 2006.

13- While the original intention was that the two Alsace churches would be identical, such is not the case. For reasons of economy, modifications were made. The brick Oley Reformed (U.C.C.) church remains much the same as when constructed. In 1909, the Lutherans erected a more modern structure on the site of the building shown.

14- Berks County's Galen Hall and the one at Atlantic City were originally owned by the same corporation. Local "march king" Monroe A. Althouse wrote a sprightly march named "Overland," in praise of the once popular automobile.

15- Hinnershitz Church, now known as Church of the Good Shepherd, had a union congregation at the time of this rendering. In more recent years, it's been a U.C.C. church. A huge Christopher Shearer oil painting adorns the front wall of the sanctuary.

16- Like most of the resorts on Neversink, the Highland House was destroyed in a spectacular fire in 1930. Until around 1908, an incline plane carried guests from 13th and Fairview St. to the summit level. Schwartz's Summit Hotel was razed in 1959. In its later years, teenaged dances were hosted here by the Police Athletic League.

17- Into the 1960's, Reading operated a fine playground system, bolstered by a Playground Federation that sponsored activities throughout the summer. One of the early playgrounds in the city was conducted beneath the Penn Street Viaduct.

18- Zion-Reed's Lutheran congregation possesses three antique organs, one being a Gruber Organ manufactured in Stouchsburg, walking distance from the church. Trinity Church in Mt. Penn had a Mount Penn-made Palm organ, which no longer survives. The building shown was replaced by a large modern structure-during Rev. Sterner's tenure.

19- Most of the statuary and ornamental urns in City Park were made of iron. Virtually all were given to the World War II scrap drives, including the once much-admired Elk Fountain.

20- In architect Alexander Forbes Smith's memoirs, which I read many years ago, he makes clear reference to *his* having designed the bandstand. Puzzling!

21- The bicycle track in the park was the same course once used for horse racing during the era, prior to 1887, that the Berks County Fair was held in Penn's Common. Among the city's best-known bicyclists was Emil Neubling, for many years operator of a Penn Street sporting goods store.

22- Highway travel through this section followed the Centre Turnpike, as there was no North Fifth Street prior to the 1890's. In the foreground of this sketch was, from the earliest years of the town, a huge gorge or depression in the earth. For many decades, a conscious effort was made to fill in it so that 5th Street could be opened north of this point. Coal-stove ash was the principal fill.

23- The former Woodward Street Market building still stands as a plumbing supply facility. Old timers might recall that for a number of years, the structure served as a roller-skating rink. As the building is not visible from 5th St., many have never seen it.

24- The Hershey Building was destroyed by fire soon after its construction. That Milton Hershey had an early presence in Reading is generally unknown as his name rarely appeared in print. His business was identified as the Lancaster Caramel Company. The splendid Lyric Theatre later occupied the site, but it too burned to the ground-in 1925.

25- Newspapers of the period made much of the fact "A Day's Hunt" was sold for the most money ever paid to a living American painter for a still life -$4,800. For many years this was owned by Reading's Sternbergh family. The Historical Society of Berks County has a lion painting which some speculate was a trial rendering and never actually completed.

26- The elk statue that once graced the front yard was the creation of Reading sculptor Oreste Brunicardi of North 8th St., near Luden's. Supposedly, when the order moved its headquarters to Hampden Blvd., the metallic statue broke into small pieces that couldn't be reassembled. The elk that replaced it is plastic!

27- The north end of the flatiron building served for many years as a branch of the Pennsylvania Bank. The "New Armory" was one of Reading's main public venues for dances and entertainments. In its latter days, it was housed a Food Fair market. A parking lot marks the site.

28- The fairgrounds in 1904, at 11th and City Line with entrance on 11th facing the Fairview Brewery, is the same plot of land now occupied by Reading's main post office.

29- The gymnasium building on Kutztown University's campus--renamed in honor of Walter Risley, longtime physical education professor–is scheduled for eventual demolition.

30- The piano player seen in the Lichty ad was a Rube Goldberg contrivance that never caught on as a practical amusement. You'd insert a perforated (piano) roll into the mechanism which was then carefully pushed against the piano keyboard. Felt-covered dowel rods were the fingers that played the keys. The slightest shift of position between the two units resulted in cacophony!

31- Early on and for a brief period, the Berkshire County Club operated in Wyomissing. Louie Heizmann, a former president of the Historical Society of Berks County, recalled in the twilight of his years playing golf in Wyomissing and hitting the ball parallel to Penn Avenue–on the south side.

32- The dancing pavilion was converted to the Carsonia Theatre, which had its own theatrical stock company for a number of years.

33- Year after year, in an effort to generate public enthusiasm, new attractions were added yearly and were widely advertised long before the season's opening. As a general rule, the amounts quoted in the press as being spent for the latest attraction was about double the amount actually expended. Nearly everyone thought the Old Mill's waterwheel moved the water and the boats. Actually, the water moved the wheel as it wasn't attached to any mechanism!

34- The big push for construction of the Spring Street Subway was the concern for school children who regularly crossed the railroad tracks at grade level to and from school. Readingites are all too familiar with the Subway's constant flooding, brought about by surreptitiously substituting smaller drainage pipes than called for in the original plans. The flooding problem was largely rectified in more recent years.

35- The same plan for an overhead bridge was once proposed for Reading's 7th and Penn railroad crossing. Then, it was decided that a subway might be better. In the end, costs involved either way prevented anything from being done one way or another. The Belt Line lessened Penn Street delays to some degree.

37- The Schuylkill Valley House survives as a multiple-family residence. With its porches removed and stuccoing overall, it bears little resemblance to the 19th century railroad hotel it once was.

39- For a brief period, the W.C.T.U. fountain dispensed "iced water." A low metallic door on the sidewalk side, which survives, once enclosed copper tubing that was periodically packed with ice during the hottest afternoons of summer.

40- The sketch artist of this rendering was Ellis I. Kirk, who provided the Reading Eagle with countless illustrations between 1896 and 1899. During that time, he shared drawing assignments with Kutztown art professor Henry Sheridan. Ellis died at 36 in 1907. He lies buried in Charles Evans Cemetery.

41- The 9th and South saloon was a favored Friday night haunt for Alvah Schaeffer, Tom Hannahoe's young friend and reputedly the finest cornetist in the city. He was a member of the Ringgold Band and the fellow who later played his horn over Tom's grave on Nanny Goat Hill at midnight on St. Patrick's Day.

42- The below grade-level solitary confinement cells survive-beneath the police parking lot in City Park. When the prison was torn down in 1934-37, the old cells were never removed, just filled in.

43- Cells were supplied with light and air by way of those letterbox-shaped openings which narrowed considerably from the outside wall to the upper reaches of each cell. Cells below ground level were a misery as they received little light, ventilation, or heat.

44- The top sketch is a signed Henry Sharidan rendering. While best known for his stippled oil paintings, he was an expert ceramics decorator. His ornamented porcelain dishes are highly prized. Improved social services removed the droves of hobos and tramps that prior to the 1950's were a common sight. With public assistance they could afford shelter in rooming houses.

46- City Hall in 1903 was a three-story brick building that stood on the northeast corner of 5th and Franklin, beside First Presbyterian Church. It headquartered all city departments from its erection in 1869 to 1930. Thereafter, until razed in 1946, various civic and social agencies maintained office space there.

47- To get to Reading's police department, one descended an outside stairway that led eastward from the corner of 5th and Franklin. Here, malefactors were booked, police court was held, and the lockup was located. The mayor often presided over police court.

49- Reading had a number of active "building associations" that aggressively built the row homes for which the city is recognized throughout the country. The first building association was organized in 1876, and in the decade that followed, 800 city row homes-erected a block at a time-were the result. Louis Kremp, the driving force of that movement, organized an impressive number of associations and served as secretary for most of them.

50- Periodically, widespread illnesses overtook the city, often borne of vermin that thrived under unsanitary conditions. To combat the filth problem, residents often worked together to clean "their block," alleyways and gutters especially. Years ago, it was common practice to indiscriminately strew the gutters and alleys with cigar butts, garbage--and worse.

52- Water can still be seen draining through the rocks at the site of the White House Spring, located on the east side of the South 9th Street extension, just above City Line.

55 or 56-The group of men that owned Stoudt's steadfastly refused to sell its bridge to the county at its assessed value. The situation changed when the county threatened to build a new bridge and relocate the roadways to the new bridge.

57- This corner played a significant part in the early history of Readingtowne, as for decades the pubic whipping post was situated between the front door of the middle structure *(top view)* and the curb-line. The "Fashion," though modified cosmetically over the years, survived a century until razed to make way for the recently constructed Sovereign headquarters.

58- D. Elmer Dampman, contractor and builder, was a prosperous businessman with a two-room office suite in the Baer Building and a fine home at 315 South 5th. He was a Reading councilman from 1887 to 1895.

59- The Mt. Sunset School, now a residence along the east side of Grand View Rd. between Wernersville and Caron Foundation (Chit-Chat) headquarters, was visited by school officials from all over Pennsylvania. It was Berks' first Standard School, meaning it had proper desks/seating, slate blackboards, modern maps and books, and individual drinking cups for each pupil. Running spring water was supplied from Grand View Sanatorium. It was the only one-room schoolhouse in Berks with "an automatic furnace" thermostatically regulated. Clarence Deppen, its teacher, was a highly regarded educator. Wyomissing School is now home to Institute of the Arts. Longswamp built the first consolidated school in Berks on "church hill." The building was removed years ago. Shillington School, remodeled for present-day office use, was built around the earlier building on the site.

60- Prior to establishment of Mt. Penn Borough, this settlement straddling the Perkiomen Turnpike, was identified as Dengler's or Woodvale. The three structures shown all passed into history decades ago. The original one-room schoolhouse that served the turnpike-area residents survives as a beauty parlor at 2319 Perkiomen Ave. Faith Lutheran, formerly along 23rd St., was one of three Lutheran churches built from the *same plans*. The other two were original Hope Lutheran (on Schuylkill Ave. near Greenwich) and Peace at 1728 Centre Ave. From the exterior, the latter two survive much as when built.

61- Transit officials encouraged development of "trolley suburbs" to increase ridership. Long after Laureldale became a recognized entity, Rosedale School and the Rosedale Knitting Mill retained their original names. Speedway Park paralleled Lancaster Ave. on the north side in the first block of East Lancaster Ave.

62- Glenside is the most enduring of all the suburban development names, attributable in large measure to the enduring presence of the Glenside Homes, long spoken of as "the Glenside [housing] Project." Until Glenside was annexed by the city, Bern Township extended southward to the Schuylkill River.

63- The Rosenbaum Store was rebuilt into an architecturally complex and intriguing structure last occupied as the A.S. Beck shoe store; see illustration on page 69. Gring's Furniture Store remains relatively unchanged. The C. K. Whitner complex, partly shown, burned completely in 1911.

64- George Britton's Store, which eventually occupied 400 to 404 Penn St., was for a period one of Reading's major department stores. The huge "Britton's" billboard atop Mt. Penn was shown on a mammoth theatrical backdrop depicting City Park, which was created by Clint Shilling for the Astor Theatre. That rolled-up "canvas" remained in the theater until its razing.

65- Long known as the Colonial Trust Building, this remains one of the finest structures in the city. Visitors to the site admire the varied and splendid ornamentation on all levels above the first floor. The "American Bank Annex," extending northward along 5th St., shows scenes from local history in the form of sculptured brick.

66- The most distinctive feature of the Baer Building, situated above the Court Street entrance, is a handsome half-relief sculpture of a bear's head. Long before both the Baer and Colonial Trust buildings was what most old-timers called Reading's first skyscraper, Jacob Mishler's 6-level Grand Central Hotel at 405-411 Penn, erected in 1861. It was razed in 1931 to make way for an Acme supermarket.

67- The portico (canopy) over the sidewalk at the Railroad Hotel, northeast corner of 7th and Penn (Read's Dept. Store site), was one of many that once fronted stores on the north side of Penn Street between 4th and 10th. Porticos were constructed to allow merchants to display goods out in the open, yet "under roof," for passersby to examine. Large "show windows" reduced the need for outdoor displays.

68- Regrettably, the Klapperthal Pavilion was built on the sunny side of Neversink which received few breezes during the tourist season. Those who came usually never came back! All components of this huge structure were salvaged for home construction in Mount Penn.

69- Notice the Rosenbaum/A. S. Beck shoe store building on the southeast corner of 7th and Penn. Into the 1950's, locals often wondered why a footbridge was never built over the tracks at this point. Completion of the Belt-Line around Reading in 1902, on the west side of the Schuylkill, did reduce the number of trains crossing Penn Street-but not enough!

70- The large industrial complex seen on the right (east) side of the bridge was Keystone Furnace, a part of the Reading Iron Company. Notice the Schuylkill Canal running along the east (Reading) shore.

71- Pennsylvania Trust, in 1904 headquartered at 536 Penn, had branches all over the city during this period. On the north end of the flatiron building where 8th and 9th streets join, just north of Spring, Pennsylvania Trust still appears cut into stone above the doorway.

72- The Mount Penn Stove Works factory survives at what was designated as 3rd & Lebanon Valley R.R., which was on N. 3rd St., south side of Greenwich. Like Reading's brewers years ago, many local bakers a century ago were German, most of whom learned their trade at Schofer's.

73- Group photos of local hosiery mill employees show large numbers of girls between the ages of 14 and 16. In the era when pupils could quit school at age 14 or the end of 8th grade, many girls left for mill jobs to help support the family.

74- Some of Reading's cigar "factories" were mom-and-pop operations conducted in some room in their homes, i.e., a cottage industry! The first floor front of Julius Hansen's factory, southwest corner of 10th and Spring, was converted in 1912 to house Hansen's Gem Theater, a silent-movie house. It closed eight years later when the handsome Strand Theatre opened at 9th and Spring.

75- An vintage newspaper notice of the Prospect Dye Works advertised that "Your Dyeing is our Living." Other local dyers and scourers included W. H. Kohl, 307 Penn; Liberty, 206 Mifflin; Neversink, 929 Muhlenberg; and O. F. Thiry, 43 N. 9th. All were greatly affected by the World War I embargo that cut off supplies of high-quality German dyes.

76- Streetcorner newspaper sellers were particularly successful when "extra" editions were printed to announce major news events too good to hold hours longer until the next regular edition. Extras ceased to exist with the coming of radio that broke news stories the minute they were reported.

77- During this era, the *Reading Eagle* circulation soared. Nearly everyone attempted to see a paper daily as it was the only way to know what was happening at home and away.

78- In 1868 the *Reading Daily and Weekly Eagle* operation opened in the former Schmucker Hotel building at the southwest corner of 6th and Penn. As circulation increased and newer machinery was obtained, larger and more substantial accommodations had to be obtained. Heavy linotype machines and large presses became too great for the old building with its aging timber-joists and rafters to support. The 6th and Cherry annex was the answer.

•

88